T0029655

DISCOVERING
LONDON'S
CANALS

ON FOOT, BY BIKE OR BY BOAT

DISCOVERING
LONDON'S
CANALS

ON FOOT, BY BIKE OR BY BOAT

Derek Pratt and Richard Mayon-White

**ADLARD
COLES**

LONDON • OXFORD • NEW YORK • NEW DELHI • SYDNEY

ADLARD COLES
Bloomsbury Publishing Plc
50 Bedford Square, London, WC1B 3DP, UK
29 Earlsfort Terrace, Dublin 2, Ireland

BLOOMSBURY, ADLARD COLES and the Adlard Coles logo are trademarks
of Bloomsbury Publishing Plc

First published in 1977 in Great Britain as *Discovering London's Canals* by
Shire Publications Ltd.
This edition published 2023

Copyright © Derek Pratt and Richard Mayon-White, 2023

Derek Pratt and Richard Mayon-White have asserted their right under the Copyright,
Designs and Patents Act, 1988, to be identified as Author of this work

All rights reserved. No part of this publication may be reproduced or transmitted in
any form or by any means, electronic or mechanical, including photocopying,
recording, or any information storage or retrieval system, without prior permission
in writing from the publishers

Bloomsbury Publishing Plc does not have any control over, or responsibility for, any third-
party websites referred to or in this book. All internet addresses given in this book were
correct at the time of going to press. The author and publisher regret any inconvenience
caused if addresses have changed or sites have ceased to exist, but can accept no
responsibility for any such changes

A catalogue record for this book is available from the British Library

Library of Congress Cataloguing-in-Publication data has been applied for

ISBN: PB: 978-1-3994-0426-6; epub: 978-1-3994-0425-9; ePDF: 978-1-3994-0424-2

2 4 6 8 10 9 7 5 3 1

Design by by Susan McIntyre. Typeset in 10 on 13pt Athelas
Maps by Richard Thomson
Printed and bound in India by Replika Press Pvt. Ltd.

MIX
Paper from
responsible sources
FSC® C016779

To find out more about our authors and books visit www.bloomsbury.com
and sign up for our newsletters

Contents

- London's other waterway   7
- The Grand Union main line: Brentford to Denham   12
- The Slough Arm   34
- The Paddington Canal   38
- The Regent's Canal   66
- The Limehouse Cut   98
- The Lee Navigation: Bow to Waltham   104
- Some other London waterways   121
- Conclusion   123
- Further reading   124
- Useful addresses   125
- Index   126

Albert Bridge on the River Thames.

London's other waterway

The River Thames is one of the world's best-known rivers and, without it, London would probably not have existed. The city first took shape on the banks of the river, gradually spreading out as its population and prosperity increased. During the 18th century the Industrial Revolution caused the expansion of towns and cities in other parts of Britain. London was left virtually out of touch with the new manufacturing centres in the Midlands and the North. Cities such as Birmingham and Sheffield had no major river by which to transport their manufactured goods or receive raw materials; the only method of transport was via primitive roads that were no better than rutted, potholed tracks, making it almost impossible to bring in raw materials and safely distribute finished goods. It was essential for the manufacturing towns to be linked to the ports and the solution was to build canals.

The first canal to be independent of a river was built near Manchester by the Duke of Bridgewater in 1761. Afterwards the introduction of the pound lock made it possible for canals to negotiate gradients – although the early canal engineers tended to follow land contours whenever possible. In the following 50 years canals were constructed all over Britain.

The Oxford Canal, completed in 1790, made the first connection between the industrial areas of the Midlands and the North to the River Thames. From Oxford, the boatmen still had a tortuous journey downriver to the capital. London's first direct link with the waterways of the Midlands began with the construction of the Grand Junction Canal at the turn of the 19th century. The link with the Thames at Brentford was complete by 1800, cutting over 60 miles (100km) off the earlier journey via Oxford and avoiding the necessity for transhipment to barges. The new Grand Junction locks were twice the width of those on the narrow Oxford Canal, which meant they could take wide barges or two narrowboats side by side. Soon the Paddington Arm brought the Grand Junction Canal nearer to central London, followed by the Regent's Canal in 1820 making the connection with the docks in East London. Although the canals arrived relatively late in London, commerce via the waterways lasted longer in the capital than in many other parts of Britain when faced with railway competition. Three million tons of cargo were moved on London's canals in 1924. Coal, timber, sand, gravel and groceries were the main cargoes at that time.

The River Lee Navigation starts at Hertford and takes a southerly route through north and east London to join the Thames at Canning Town. It has two direct links with the Regent's Canal, which runs from Limehouse to Paddington. The Paddington Arm heads out across north-west London to Southall, where it joins the main line at Bulls Bridge. There is a branch near Uxbridge that runs to Slough. The main line continues through Uxbridge and heads out over the Chiltern Hills to Birmingham and the rest of England. From the centre of London, it is possible to travel by boat to places as far afield as Lincoln, Llangollen, Gloucester and Goole. Major cities such as Manchester, Leeds, Nottingham, Bristol and Coventry are all accessible by canal from London.

There was considerably more green countryside to be seen when London's canals were first built. Suburbs such as Hanwell and Southall were mere villages separated by farms and fields. The canal attracted industry to its banks. Factories and foundries were built with waterside wharves where boats could load and unload their cargoes. The canals continued to function as busy commercial waterways right up to the 1960s, carrying such varied cargoes as coal, timber, sand, chemicals and domestic rubbish. The shipment of raw lime juice in barrels from Brentford to Rose's factory at Apsley in Hertfordshire, which ended in 1981, was the last regular commercial narrowboat run on the southern Grand Union until 2003, when a gravel barge contract began operating between Denham and West Drayton.

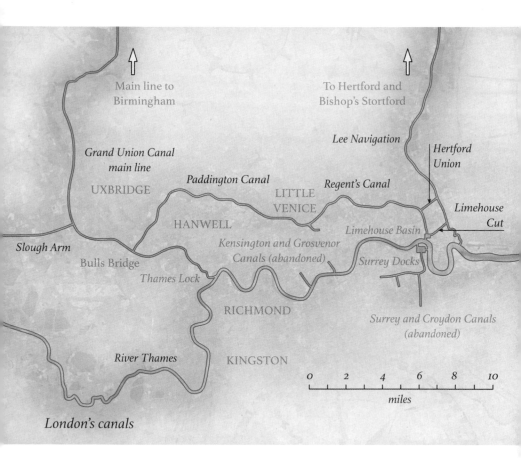

London's canals

The people who worked the narrowboats had a way of life that was totally dependent on the canals. They had to labour extremely hard, especially in winter when the water was frozen. The boatman and his family lived and slept in the tiny, cramped cabins behind the cargo hold at the back of the boats. Because they were an itinerant community, they were often regarded with suspicion by land-based people and so became isolated from the rest of society. With the decline of trade, the families gradually drifted away from the canal to work in factories or to retirement, though a few did manage to stay on as lock keepers or maintenance men. Now there is a new generation of canal dwellers on the growing number of residential boats.

Start of Regent's Canal near Little Venice.

The canals are commemorated by the names of streets and pubs around London. Besides Canal Streets and Wharf Roads, there is Praed Street in Paddington named after William Praed, the first chairman of the Grand Junction Canal Company. Pub signs include the Grand Junction Arms, the Narrow Boat, the Pleasure Boat and the Paddington Packet Boat.

Most of the boats now seen on London's canals are privately owned or are public trip boats. Trip boats are to be found on the very popular section of canal between Little Venice and Camden Lock. Indeed, arriving at London Zoo by boat is the most attractive way to travel to see the animals.

Hired holiday boats from outside the capital are often seen during the summer months. There is a fleet of hire boats at Packet Boat Marina at Cowley Peachey. Canoes and kayaks are popular and are available at clubs and watersports centres.

In 1968, Westminster City Council was the first local authority to provide a canal walk for public use. This ran between Primrose Hill and Lisson Grove. Before this walkway opened, the public had been actively discouraged from using the towpath, with access often denied at bridges. All the canal towpaths are now open and their use is both encouraged and promoted. Hidden beneath the towpath are electricity and fibre-optic cables, which bring in revenue to the Canal & River Trust. Information boards about the canal and its history are displayed in many places.

There are many changes occurring alongside London's canals. There have been major developments at Paddington, King's Cross, Brentford, and along the Paddington Canal. Perhaps the biggest transformation has been in London's East End, around the lower Lee Navigation as a result of the 2012 Olympic Games. New building continues, much of it making good use of the waterside.

London's canals are now part of the Grand Union Canal system and the River Lee Navigation, both owned and managed by the Canal & River Trust. There are traces of other canals to be found but these are long abandoned and mostly infilled.

This book is for people who want to discover the canals of London on foot. Most people's awareness of the canals ends at Camden Lock or London Zoo at Regent's Park, but there are about 60 miles (100km) of London's waterways waiting to be explored by visitors who want to look further than the obvious tourist attractions. All the walks described in this book are north of the Thames.

The Grand Union main line

Brentford to Denham

13½ miles (21.5km) with 15 locks (including Denham Deep Lock)

Hanwell Locks.

Canal highlights

- Brentford Gauging Locks
- Glaxo Smith Kline building
- Hanwell Flight of Locks
- Bulls Bridge
- Stockley Park
- Packet Boat Marina
- Cowley Lock
- Denham Deep Lock with Fran's Tea Garden

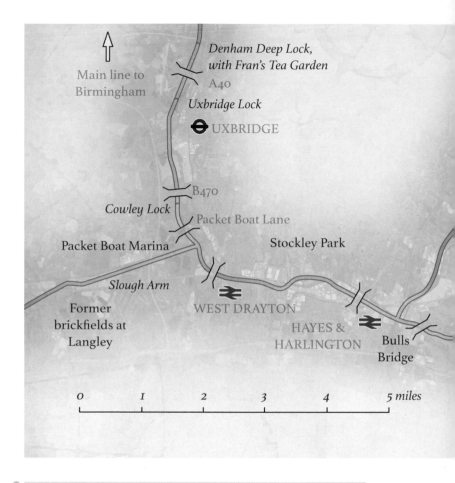

Main line to
Birmingham

Denham Deep Lock,
with Fran's Tea Garden
A40

Uxbridge Lock

⊖ UXBRIDGE

B470

Cowley Lock

Packet Boat Lane

Packet Boat Marina

Stockley Park

Slough Arm

Former
brickfields at
Langley

WEST DRAYTON

HAYES &
HARLINGTON

Bulls
Bridge

0   1   2   3   4   5 miles

HISTORY

The Grand Junction Canal between Brentford and Uxbridge
was opened in November 1794 with celebrations and processions
along its length. At that time the present Brentford Lock (lock
No 100) was the last one on the canal and boats were subject to
delay in navigating the tidal Brent Creek. The Thames Lock was
eventually constructed once opposition from millers using the
water in the creek had been overcome. The River Brent joins the
main line at the bottom of Hanwell Locks and is then canalised
down to the Thames at Brentford.

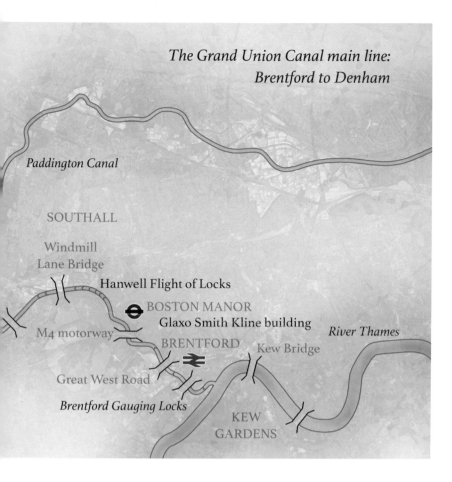

*The Grand Union Canal main line:
Brentford to Denham*

Paddington Canal

SOUTHALL

Windmill
Lane Bridge

Hanwell Flight of Locks

BOSTON MANOR
Glaxo Smith Kline building

River Thames

M4 motorway

BRENTFORD   Kew Bridge

Great West Road

Brentford Gauging Locks

KEW
GARDENS

In 1929 the Grand Junction Canal main line was amalgamated with the Paddington Arm, the Regent's Canal and all the lines to Birmingham, Leicester and near Nottingham to form the Grand Union Canal. The new Grand Union Canal became the most extensive canal in Britain and carried an immense quantity of goods. Railway competition eventually affected the overall tonnages – although the Grand Union did not suffer as much as did some other waterways. Brentford with its transhipment depot remained a very busy terminal to the canal until the 1970s. Development at the start of the 21st century has caused big changes in the Brentford area, and it is here that we shall begin our walk.

BRENTFORD TO HANWELL   (4 miles, 6.5km)

Start at Thames Lock, which is the entrance from the Thames to the Grand Union Canal. *The nearest station is Brentford (National Rail from Waterloo) ½ mile (1km) away. At the station turn left on to Boston Manor Road and continue along Half Acre. At the High Street turn left and cross to Dock Road, a small, cobbled cul-de-sac on the right. At the end of the road, a path goes between boatyards to the lock.*

At the footbridge over Thames Lock, you can look down at the tidal Brent Creek with the Thames and Kew Gardens in the distance. The double lock is operated by a resident lock keeper and boat access is dependent on the state of the tide. The second chamber was added in 1962, along with electrification of the lock operation, when the creek was busy with barges and lighters. The former Brentford Railway Dock has its own separate entrance to the Thames, upstream of Brent Creek. It is now a marina that is surrounded by a large housing development. The marina can be seen beyond Thames Lock.

From the footbridge, walk down the steps to the path on the far side of the lock (left side if looking upstream). The way is signposted as the Grand Union Canal Walk and the Thames Path. Cross the canal at the next footbridge and walk under the bridge that used to carry the track to the railway dock and is now the road into the marina. You can either follow the Thames Path signs past the entrance to a timber yard or take a slightly longer canalside route signed to the residential boats and to Brent Way. This canalside route requires a climb over a low wall that is a flood defence. Both ways bring you to Brentford Bridge and High Street. The buildings by the former railway bridge were being reconstructed when the book was written, so do be aware that the path and signage may change.

Cross the High Street to find the Grand Union Canal Walk and the Capital Ring Path signposted at the end of the bridge

Thames Lock at Brentford.

nearest the Holiday Inn. The hotel has a bar with indoor and outside seating overlooking the Brentford Gauging Locks and the tollhouse where traffic coming from the Thames was assessed for the value of its cargo. Up until 2003, when they were demolished, you would have seen the warehouses of Brentford Transhipment Depot. The depot was once a bustling scene of industry with barges and lighters from the Thames mingling with canal boats. Cranes would have been loading and unloading all types of cargo from one craft to another or into lorries. Following the decline of canal trade in the early 1960s, the depot continued to operate as a storage place for freight from the Thames. By the mid-1980s this trade had ceased and the depot fell into disuse. The area has been transformed since by the construction of new houses, the hotel, a piazza area with waterside bars, a reedbed for wildlife, and improved flood protection measures.

Brentford Gauging Locks.

Walk down to the footpath to the Gauging Locks, noticing the first of the Grand Junction canal mileposts, telling you that Braunston is 93 miles (150km) away. Braunston, a village near Daventry in Northamptonshire, is the hub of the canal system south of Birmingham. It has long been an important canal centre for working boats and pleasure boating, and it has a junction with the Oxford Canal.

After the locks, the path turns left around the office of the Canal & River Trust, which has put up excellent information boards. Immediately, you will see the glass, cathedral-like Glaxo Smith Kline (GSK) building on the horizon. After the apartments, the towpath goes through the roofless remains of a huge warehouse that had canopies over the canal. This is where perishable cargoes could be handled with protection from the weather. The allotments on the opposite bank give a feeling of timelessness.

Passing the GSK building at
Great West Road, Brentford.

There are a number of modern office buildings near the Great
West Road bridge, all impressive in their own right, but all are
overshadowed by the GSK offices, which have a garden area with
a large colourful sculpture and seats where workers can sit out by
the canal in their leisure time.

A wooden footbridge connects the towpath to Boston Manor
Park, where there is a 17th-century manor house and gardens.
Round the corner lies Clitheroe's Lock, probably named after
former owners of Boston Manor. On the offside, the elevated
M4 motorway looms over the River Brent before a left-hand
bend takes the canal to pass under Gallows Bridge. Built in the
Midlands by the Horseley Iron Works, this is one of the finest
canal bridges in the south of England. Cast-iron bridges of this
type are very common around the canals of the West Midlands but
are rarely found this far south. The bridge has been painted and

Gallows Bridge.

the anomaly of 'Grand Union Canal 1820' rectified. The original inscription correctly read 'Grand Junction Canal' but was later foolishly altered to 'Grand Union Canal', a name that did not exist until 1929. This is a roving bridge designed to enable boat horses and walkers to cross the canal when the towpath changes sides.

The Heathrow branch of the Piccadilly line of the London Underground crosses the canal on a high metal bridge. The canal is wooded on both sides and then it passes under the M4 motorway and arrives at Osterley Lock. The lock is situated next to mature woodland between the canal and the River

Brent and only the noise of the motorway traffic disturbs the tranquillity of the scene. Look for the charming mosaics set in brickwork on the ground beside the lock and made by children from a nearby school.

Beyond the lock the River Brent leaves the canal and plunges over a large toothed weir. Rising sharply behind the river is the Elthorne extension, part of the Brent River Park that lies on the banks of the River Brent as far as Perivale. The Elthorne extension has playing fields, wildlife reserves and a large sculpture of a deer (known locally as the 'Elthorne Bambi') set rather incongruously

Hanwell Bottom Lock.

next to a football pitch. *This is the nearest point to Boston Manor station (Underground – Piccadilly line). To reach it, cross the football pitches to Southdown Avenue, turn right to the end of the avenue, then left into the main road. The station is on the right.*

A pleasant half-mile amble takes you to Hanwell Locks. There is an orchard, the Piggeries, planted beside the towpath on what was a small dock. This dock became disused and was replaced by a smallholding that gave its name to the orchard. The River Brent enters the canal under a bridge on the towpath side just before the bottom lock. The Fox Inn pub can be found a short distance along the lane before the bridge. In 1897 the Brent was so polluted it was described as an open sewer and boatmen complained of the stench caused by filth stirred up by their loaded boats. These days a resident heron and the occasional kingfisher are living proof that fish have returned to the Brent.

A WALK TO BUNNY PARK

(2 miles/3km)

▲ *Wharncliffe Viaduct.*

To explore a little more of the Brent Valley Park, at the bottom Hanwell lock follow the Fitzherbert Walk by the river Brent to Hanwell Bridge. Cross the road under a pedestrian subway and carry on into Brent Meadow with the river on your right. The Wharncliffe or Hanwell railway viaduct looms up in front of you. This was built by Isambard Kingdom Brunel in 1837 and carries the Great Western Railway from Paddington to the West Country.

Cross the river over a little bridge directly underneath the viaduct and pass through a gate into a steep grassy area known as Churchfields. *To reach Hanwell station (National Rail to Paddington), walk up the slope and turn right at the top. Follow a track between a public garden and the railway viaduct to a road junction. Go straight ahead along Golden Manor and turn right into Campbell Road. Follow this to the end and bear right to the station entrance.*

To continue the walk to Bunny Park, go up the slope and turn left along a beautiful avenue of chestnut trees to St Mary's Church, which was built by Gilbert Scott. Turn left in front of the church and enter Brent Lodge Park (popularly known as the 'Bunny Park'). Follow the path to a zoo, where there is also an excellent café, a maze and an adventure playground. Return to the canal by the same route.

▶ *The spire of St Mary's Church, Hanwell.*

There are several splendid walks around here. Jubilee Meadow and Blackberry Corner, unspoilt wild spaces, can be found by crossing the lock. Here one can well imagine the open countryside in this area before the locks were built in 1794. Next to the towpath is another path indicating the entrance to Fitzherbert Walk, part of the Brent River Park, which runs for 6 miles (9.5km) between the A40 Western Avenue and Brentford High Street.

HANWELL TO HAYES   (3½ miles, 5.5km)

Back at the canal, there are six locks in the Hanwell Flight, raising the canal by 53 feet (16m). Around 60,000 gallons (270,000 litres) are lost at each lock with every boat movement up the flight. A high wall on the towpath side separates the canal from Ealing Hospital grounds and the former Hanwell Asylum (later known as St Bernard's Hospital). Note the bricked-up arch in the wall between Locks 93 and 94. This was once the entrance to Asylum Dock through which boats delivered coal for the hospital's boilers. Lock 94 is still known as 'Asylum Lock'. The red-painted doors set into the wall are fire doors that allowed fire engines to extract water from the canal if a blaze occurred in the hospital. Sometimes a boat horse would slip into the water when pulling a heavy load and horse ramps helped them escape where the canal has a steep side. These can still be seen at Hanwell Locks and along the Regent's Canal.

The next bridge is the renowned 'Three Bridges', where road, rail and canal cross at the same point at different levels. Three Bridges is actually one bridge and an aqueduct. Brunel built the railway in 1859 and a section of his broad-gauge rail can be seen acting as a bridge guard on the southern side of the aqueduct. The Glade Lane Canalside Park is another of Ealing's many open spaces. Only the garden wall survives of the fine lock cottage at Lock 91, which is sometimes counted as a seventh Hanwell lock. The cottage was demolished and the debris is overgrown with wildflowers.

A splendid whitewashed bridge frames the entrance to Norwood Top Lock, where the Canal & River Trust has an office and maintenance yard. Now begins a long stretch of canal between locks, known as a pound, extending to Cowley Lock near Uxbridge on the main line and along the Paddington and Regent's Canals as far as Camden Lock. Add to this the Slough Arm (see page 34) and there is a distance of around 27 miles (43km) of water uninterrupted by locks. Note the lock and bridge competition plaques indicating that the lock has won prizes for being well kept.

After the lock the towpath rises over the entrance to the Maypole Arm, which ran for ½ mile (1km) to Maypole Dock. It was built in 1913 to serve the Mønsted margarine works and later the Quaker Oats factory. It is used for private moorings and is not open to the public.

Bixley Triangle is a small sculpture park and orchard that has been recovered from waste ground. A milepost here reads 'Braunston 89 miles'. Further along this long straight stretch to Wolf Bridge is The Lamb pub on the opposite side of the canal, which has a waterside garden and stands next to Norwood Road. Next the towpath crosses the entrance to Adelaide Dock, which has become a maintenance yard for the Canal & River Trust.

After you pass The Old Oak Tree pub by a brick humpback bridge and old terraced cottages, there is a large area of sports pitches called The Common. The next section of canal, between the Grand Junction Arms and Bulls Bridge, has a quiet road running parallel to it that is often used in film and television dramas.

Bulls Bridge marks the junction with the Paddington Canal, which is the water route to central London. It once faced a lively scene of working narrowboats at the Grand Union Canal Company offices and repair yards. Dozens of boats with their smoking chimneys were moored here while the boatmen awaited orders for their next job. The women would take advantage of the luxury of running water and do the family wash, while the

Bulls Bridge Junction, Grand Union main line.

children had a schoolroom in an old barge. A modern sculpture beneath Bulls Bridge commemorates the people who lived and worked on the canals and who developed their own unique community with its own costumes and customs. The bridge now faces a huge Tesco supermarket built on the site of the old depot. The supermarket has mooring facilities and a restaurant and is a popular stopping place for visiting boaters wishing to stock up their larders. There are moorings further along the canal – some of them for permanent houseboats – and also a dry-dock facility.

Beyond Bulls Bridge the busy Hayes Bypass noisily crosses the canal on concrete pillars. The large factory on the offside of the canal was occupied by Nestlé and was called 'Hayes Chocolate' by the working boatmen. 1300 new homes are being built on the site, due for completion in 2025.

The towpath rises over a short arm once known as 'Shackle's Dock' as the canal passes through Hayes town centre, with its abundance of shops and pubs. *Turn left over the canal bridge to reach Hayes & Harlington station (National Rail to Paddington), just past the shops and bus stop.*

A WALK AROUND STOCKLEY PARK   *(2½ miles/4km)*

The London Loop goes through Stockley Park, creating a circular walk when combined with the towpath. It is about equidistant (½ mile/1km) from West Drayton and Hayes & Harlington stations. The best starting place is at Weston Walk by the elegant canalside gardens in front of the Prologis buildings near Stockley Bridge. Weston Walk goes through a delightful plantation of birch and cherry trees to meet the London Loop by a bus stop called Horton Close. Cross the road, walk through a tall black kissing gate, and follow the green and white London Loop discs on trees and posts. After the elegant footbridge over the A408 road, the path goes through the golf course along a sunken lane from the 6th tee to the club house. At the club house, look for a London Loop finger post and more discs on trees to find the way. When the path reaches a collection of office buildings, pause to admire the architecture of The Square and to enjoy the peaceful scene by the small lake and waterfall. Another London Loop finger post points the way along a short path to the canal. Walking along the canal back to Stockley Bridge will complete the circle.

HAYES TO WEST DRAYTON   (2½ miles, 4km)

The canal continues westward in a shallow cutting through an industrial area largely screened by trees and bushes. On the towpath side lies Stockley Park Science Park and Stockley Country Park, both constructed on 400 acres (162 hectares) of formerly derelict land. This was once the heart of the brickfields industry, where numerous docks were built to transport bricks and gravel to Paddington and Brentford. Now the businesses that have come in the past 30 years include hi-tech global companies. Much of the park is landscaped and it has a golf course. The proximity to Heathrow Airport is another attraction for the companies based here. On the offside, there is a large gravel and sand depot that still is a wharf, sadly not in operation in 2021.

The canal comes very close to the railway where there used to be rail-to-water transhipment sheds. Arriving in the town centre of West Drayton and Yiewsley, the canal is adorned by the Colston Bridge, which has handsome steel arches erected in 2016. This is a good stopping place with shops, pubs and West Drayton station (*National Rail to Paddington and Reading*) close by.

WEST DRAYTON TO DENHAM (3½ miles, 5.5km)

From Colston Bridge (Bridge 192) the canal has residential buildings on either side. After Trout Bridge, the canal curves to go northwards along the Colne Valley up to Rickmansworth. Soon you will see a footbridge over to the Slough Arm and the Cowley

Approaching the Cowley Peachey Junction with the Slough Arm.

Peachey Junction. Here the Packet Boat Marina was opened in 2003 and is now managed by Aquavista. It has comfortable facilities for its customers: residential and non-residential moorings, showers, laundry, Wi-Fi and good security. The entrance to this marina is at the beginning of the Slough Arm. From the Grand Union towpath, you will notice an old wharf area being used as a

Cowley Lock.

boatyard and The WatersEdge Canal Cottages, a pub with holiday accommodation and a restaurant overlooking the water by Bridge 190. Immediately opposite The WatersEdge is the bridge into what was the terminus for packet boats. This was a horse-drawn passenger service to Paddington, 15 miles (24km) away – the best transport in the early 19th century.

There are two picnic spots near Bridge 190. One is Little Britain Lake, so named because of its shape, along Packet Boat

Lane that goes over the bridge. The other is Cowley Recreation Ground, ½ mile (1km) up the towpath towards Cowley Lock. The recreation ground was created as a public space from the gardens of large houses nearby. A notice board describes the Cowley Trail of Discovery, a 2½ mile (4km) circular walk that goes up by the canal and back by the River Colne.

Cowley Lock marks the end of a lock-free section (known as a 'pound') that stretches from Camden Lock on the Paddington

Canal and Norwood Top Lock on the Grand Union. The attractive cottages by the lock include the former tollhouse which has been a tearoom. Industrial estates and moored boats lie on both sides of the canal all the way up to Bridge 184 at Uxbridge Lock, but there is plenty of interest to see. The Malt Shovel pub has been serving canal people since the early 19th century. It is at Iver Lane (Bridge 188), conveniently close to some visitors' moorings, National Cycle Route 61 and the Colne Valley Trail. The towpath crosses at this bridge to the west side of the canal, where it is joined by the London Loop long distance path as it approaches Uxbridge.

Next stop is another pub, The General Eliott in St John's Road, Uxbridge (Bridge 186). The pub's terrace faces the Hillingdon Canal Club and Uxbridge Boat Centre on the opposite bank. Uxbridge was the home of the famous canal carrying company Fellows, Morton & Clayton. Narrowboats were registered here and the legend 'Registered at Uxbridge' can be seen on old working boats. Two more attractive pubs, the Swan & Bottle and the Crown & Treaty, are close to the next bridge (Bridge 185, Oxford Road). An extraordinary art deco building in green and cream that resembles a beached ocean liner now overlooks the old pubs. Murals on the bridges are a relatively recent form of canal art. A fine example is on the inside wall of Bridge 185, where a beautiful mosaic of animals was made for London's Waterway Heritage 2000. *The centre of Uxbridge with its station (Underground – Piccadilly and Metropolitan lines), shops and cafés is only a few minutes' walk from Bridges 185 and 186.*

There is a complex series of backwaters, partly occupied by the marina Denham Yacht Station and a large flour mill at Uxbridge Lock. An attractive whitewashed roving bridge in front of the lock completes the scene. Above the lock, the canal is connected to the River Misbourne, making it wider for the next ⅔ mile (1km). Houses with waterside gardens and the green spaces in the modern Uxbridge Business Park show that the canal is leaving London. Once past the wide A40 bridge, you are in open

Denham Deep Lock.

countryside. Cross over the canal on Bridge 183 and soon you are at Denham Deep Lock, the end of our walk by the Grand Union Canal main line. You deserve refreshment at Fran's Tea Garden behind the pretty lock cottage. Sitting in this idyllic garden on a sunny day, it is hard to believe that you are 2 miles (3km) inside the circle of the M25 motorway.

Just before Denham Lock, a footpath signposted as the South Bucks Way goes from the towpath to Denham Country Park with its visitor centre, café (good to know if Fran's Tea Garden is closed) and car parking. The distance is ⅓ mile (0.5km). It is a great place, where children can explore and cycle safely among trees and meadows. A walk of 1½ miles (2.5km) along the South Bucks Way will take you into Denham Village and to the station, with trains to Marylebone and High Wycombe (Chiltern Railways).

The Slough Arm

5 miles (8km), no locks

Canal highlights

- Packet Boat Marina
- Former brickfields at Langley
- Canalside park at Slough

Peace on the Slough Arm.

HISTORY

The Slough Arm was built in 1882, making it one of the last canals completed in Britain. Its main purpose was to transport bricks for building the expanding suburbs of London in the late Victorian era. When the brickfields were exhausted, gravel pits supplied the main trade along the arm. Now the gravel pits have become fishing lakes and this offshoot of the Grand Union is a peaceful backwater. The canal runs in straight east to west, with the towpath on its south side.

COWLEY PEACHEY TO SLOUGH (5 miles, 8km)

When going along the Slough Arm from the Grand Union at Cowley Peachey, the first thing that you will notice is the entrance to the Packet Boat Marina (see page 125). A wooden footbridge (Bridge 0) is a way into the marina through a gate that is unlocked in daylight hours. The landscaped grounds of the marina make a pleasant start to the first mile, which is green and wooded. The canal passes over three aqueducts above three side streams of the River Colne, of which the most significant is Colne Brook. At Trout Lane bridge (Bridge 1), a large stone marks the boundary of the City of London, now the dividing line between Hillingdon and Slough. This bridge carries the Colne Valley Trail and the London Loop over the canal and into the maze of lakes and streams on either side.

Passing under the M25 motorway, you enter a cutting where trees screen industrial estates and muffle the traffic noise. Iver lies on the north side of the canal, but its station is to the south along Thorney Lane (Bridge 3). After Bridge 4, the canal banks become reedy, and fields appear on both sides. A winding hole (for canal boats to turn) creates a small lake about 200 yards (182m) to the west of Bridge 4. At Mansion Lane (Bridge 6 – there is no longer a Bridge 5) lies the High Line Yachting Centre boatyard with good facilities for boaters and a long line of residential moorings up to the next bridge. There are a few other boats along the rest of the Slough Arm. At

The Slough Arm.

Bridge 7, Station Road leads to Langley station, shops and cafés if you want a midway break. Going on towards Slough, the south side of the canal has industry and warehouses. On the north side, there used to be brickfields but their remains are covered by grass, shrubs and a golf course. National Cycle Route 41, the Colne Valley Trail and a path to Langley Country Park cross Bridge 8, with its iron lattice sides so like the aqueducts earlier along the way.

The last 1½ miles (2.5km) to Slough are a pleasant walk. The water is fringed by reeds, the houses have canalside gardens, a recreational park has good information boards, and the nearby industry is light. There is evidence of litter picking and wildflowers sowing by the Friends of Slough Canal (www.friendsofsloughcanal.com). The canal ends at Stoke Road (B470) by the Shaggy Calf Lane bus stop. Turn left on Stoke Road to reach Slough station (*National Rail to Paddington and Reading*) and the town centre.

At the time of writing, we thought that more could be done to attract visitors here, starting with better signage and a clearly visible information board. The Slough Arm was once part of an ambitious plan to link the Grand Union Canal with the River Thames at Maidenhead. Some optimists believe this scheme is still possible. More realistically, the Slough Arm deserves to be better known as a good walk and a quiet place to come boating.

The Paddington Canal

13 miles (21km), no locks

Paddington Basin
– approach arm.

Canal highlights

- Paddington Basin
- Little Venice
- Meanwhile Gardens
- Kensal Green Cemetery
- Park Royal
- North Circular Aqueduct
- Horsenden Hill
- Northolt Village
- Willow Tree Open Space and Marina

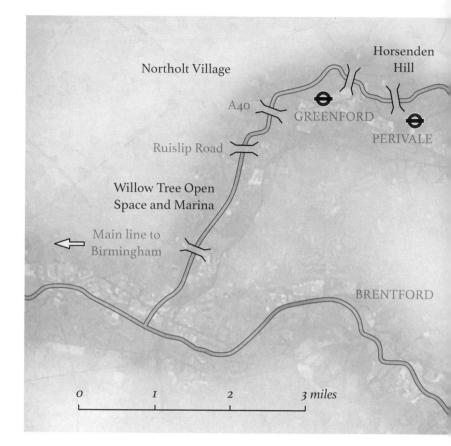

Northolt Village

Horsenden
Hill

A40

GREENFORD

PERIVALE

Ruislip Road

Willow Tree Open
Space and Marina

Main line to
Birmingham

BRENTFORD

0   1   2   3 miles

HISTORY

The Paddington Canal – or more correctly the Paddington Arm of
the Grand Junction Canal – was opened in July 1801. It provided
a direct link from the Grand Junction main line at Bulls Bridge
to Paddington in central London, thereby avoiding the River
Thames. It was built on one level so that boats could make rapid
progress unhindered by locks. Industry developed on its banks,
taking full advantage of this efficient method of transport. The
larger companies built their own wharves and private docks.

At the terminus, Paddington developed into a thriving
inland port well before it became a major railway station. In

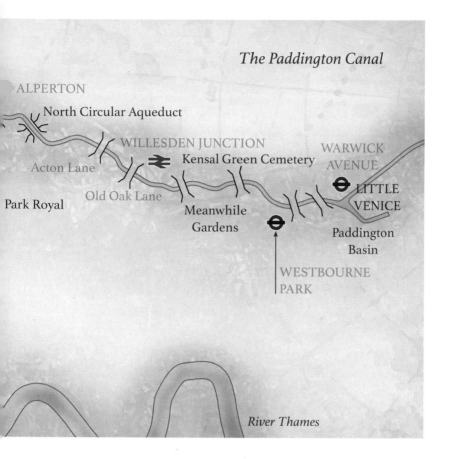

The Paddington Canal

ALPERTON

North Circular Aqueduct

WILLESDEN JUNCTION

Acton Lane

Kensal Green Cemetery

WARWICK AVENUE

LITTLE VENICE

Park Royal

Old Oak Lane

Meanwhile Gardens

Paddington Basin

WESTBOURNE PARK

River Thames

its commercial heyday, Paddington Basin was flanked with warehouses and the pool was crammed with boats loading and discharging all types of goods. Horses were everywhere, pulling carts and drays or resting in the many stables dotted around the basin. Smells from the horses and the barges full of domestic rubbish would have been overwhelming. Along the wharves, piles of sand, gravel and bricks waited to be loaded manually onto builders' carts. Local pubs such as the Grand Junction Arms were full of boatmen drinking and talking before starting work on the next load. The basin lost some of its trade to the Regent's Canal when that was built in 1820. Soon, it faced much greater competition from the railways. Nevertheless, the basin remained

Fan Bridge at Paddington Basin.

busy until the end of the Second World War. Then it declined and became a rubbish-filled backwater without public access. It is surprising that this large expanse of water, less than a mile from Marble Arch, stayed unused and derelict for half a century.

Paddington Basin was also the terminus of the Paddington Packet Boat passenger service from Cowley near Uxbridge (see page 30). Although this was the best transport system in its day, it was supplanted by the Great Western Railway (GWR) passenger service between a temporary station at Bishop's Bridge Road and Maidenhead in 1838. The present station along Eastbourne Terrace and Praed Street was designed by Brunel and opened in 1854. Now Transport for London (TfL) runs the local passenger service along the GWR route, which is convenient for walking beside the Grand Union and the Slough Arm. But, as they say, 'What goes around, comes around'. Today the most modern and most elegant entrance to Paddington station is at Paddington Basin.

In the 21st century, Paddington Basin has had three major developments. The first, Paddington Central, was built on the former Paddington station goods yard. This development combines offices, retail space and over 200 apartments. The public space is partly landscaped and decorated with modern sculpture. There is an arena for exhibitions and entertainment, and waterside restaurants and bars. The second development consists of tall blocks of offices, cafés and a hotel. Public access

Paddington Basin and entrance to Paddington station.

Little Venice.

(so long denied) has been encouraged via walkways and bridges. Three notable bridges are the unique Helix Bridge that can retract to allow boats to pass through, the elegant St Mary's Bridge into the famous hospital, and the Fan Bridge at the end of the basin. The third development, which was completed in 2021, is a waterside concourse to Paddington station through which rail passengers can walk directly to the basin.

PADDINGTON TO WILLESDEN   (3 miles, 5km)

To explore the Paddington Canal, the waterside station concourse is a good place to start. When you have finished being distracted by the cafés and boats offering river trips, walk under Westway A40, past the building known as the 'Battleship' (built in the 1960s for railway maintenance and now offices) and into Little Venice (*nearest station is Warwick Avenue: Underground – Bakerloo line*).

Canalway Cavalcade at Little Venice.

The triangular pool is the junction of the Paddington and Regent's Canals. It is reputed to have been called 'Little Venice' by the poet Robert Browning who lived nearby after his return from Italy. The small island with weeping willow trees is Browning's Island. In the summer, you can sit amid the flowers and trees of Rembrandt Gardens on the east side of the pool, watching the colourful scene. Public trip boats carry passengers to London Zoo and Camden

Lock; some have the entrance to the zoo included in the ticket. There is all manner of canal craft, varying from the beautiful to the scruffy, the functional to the elaborate. Some are restaurants, one is a theatre, another an art gallery. On the May Bank Holiday weekend each year, the Inland Waterways Association (IWA) holds the Canalway Cavalcade. This huge gathering of boats lasts three days and is a splendid celebration of London's canals.

The Paddington Canal leaves the west corner of Little Venice under a blue painted iron bridge (Bridge 3c). On the left, just beyond the bridge, is the Toll Office, known to the working boatmen as 'Paddington Stop'. Boats were stopped here to have their cargoes gauged and to be issued with toll tickets. It was a very busy place, with toll clerks working in shifts throughout the day and into the night. The office is now the London headquarters of the Canal & River Trust.

Walking along the towpath between the tree-lined Delamere Terrace and the residential boat-lined canal, you must quickly learn to be alert to passing bicycles and electric scooters. These can, and do, travel fast and silently on the hard surface of the path. The large housing complex on the towpath side is called the Warwick and Brindley Estates, built by London County Council between 1958 and 1968. The name is presumably a tribute to James Brindley, the pioneer canal engineer, although he had no connection with the Grand Junction Canal and was dead before any canal reached London. Amid the tall blocks of flats, the spire of St Mary Magdalene Church in Westbourne Green is still a landmark. The church was built in the 1870s with high arches and elaborate brickwork that was the fashion of the time. In addition to its religious purpose, it is now a heritage, cultural and arts centre for the canalside community. Westbourne is one of London's lost rivers buried in underground pipes running from Hampstead Heath to the Serpentine in Hyde Park and then to the Thames at Chelsea.

Shortly before the Harrow Road Bridge (Bridge 3), you may notice the horse ramps going down into the canal from the towpath. At the bridge itself, you can see rope grooving worn into iron plates on the corner between the side wall and the inside wall partly camouflaged by the graffiti. In the days of working boats, constant chafing of the horses' wet towing ropes gradually eroded the metal guards. Similar examples can be seen throughout the canal system.

Westbourne Green.

As you will have already observed, a walk along the Paddington Canal is a study of the good, the bad and the ugly in architecture. Rows of modern apartments on both sides of the canal lead your eyes to the soaring elevated Westway (the A40) that sweeps over the canal on its way to Oxford and Birmingham. Four generations of transport – the Great Western Railway, the Metropolitan Railway, the Westway motorway and the Paddington Canal – run side by side at this point. Carlton Bridge (Bridge 4c) is a fine cast-iron structure. Its elegant paintwork makes a contrast with the sombre-looking Union Tavern beside it. Mural paintings beneath the bridge need sunlight reflected from the water to reveal their full beauty. *Westbourne Park station (Underground – Hammersmith & City line) is close by.* On the offside of the canal, a new housing development is followed by terraced houses along the Harrow Road. Ahead, the 30-storey monolith, Trellick Tower, is one of the tallest buildings in

West London, visible for miles around. Concrete blocks like this fell out of fashion, and it is now a listed building, an example of municipal housing in the 1960s and early 1970s.

Down at ground level, the greenery and ponds in Meanwhile Gardens offer a peaceful diversion from the towpath for a few minutes. Youngsters enjoy skateboarding and other games in the adventure playground. In 1819, the area around Ladbroke Grove, then called Plough Lane, was described as 'a beautiful burst of scenery with distant views of the Hampstead Hills' (John Hassell, *A Tour of the Grand Junction Canal*). That rural idyll has long since disappeared under brick and concrete. Present-day visitors to Ladbroke Grove at the end of August will find a very lively and noisy scene at the Notting Hill Carnival, which usually starts near here.

The modern footbridge (Bridge 4ab) crosses to the Harrow Road, giving the walker access to local shops. Further along, the towpath rises sharply over what was the entrance to Kensal Wharf, also known as the 'Port-a-Bella-Dock'. The wharf was once used to load rubbish onto boats to be taken to Hayes and West Drayton to fill the holes in the quarries and brickfields. During the Second World War, the dock was drained and used to store sandbags. The arches of the wharf were shelters for air-raid rescue squads. In February 1944, the wharf was bombed and some of the original buildings were destroyed. The elegant white offices and apartments on either side of the canal are partly on top of the remains of the wharf, remembered in the building's name: Portobello Dock.

After Kensal Green Bridge (Bridge 4) at Ladbroke Grove, you will notice the wavy roof of the Boathouse Centre with its equally curvaceous sculpture by the towpath. The centre is used by young people for water-based activities with access for people with disabilities. Next door is Sainsbury's supermarket, which has temporary moorings for boaters. An unusual neighbouring building is the former water tower that was turned into a house on

Kensal Green before the gasholders were demolished.

stilts in 2005. The water tower was built in the 1930s in case of fire at the gasworks. The gasholders appeared in many photographs of this stretch of the canal, but have since gone, and the site of the gasworks is part of the Crossrail development. Beyond Sainsbury's, the towpath rises over the entrance to the gasworks wharf where huge quantities of coal from the Midlands were delivered. The last working boat to use the wharf was a tar barge from the gasworks to Beckton in east London.

Kensal Green Cemetery flanks the offside of the canal between Ladbroke Grove and Scrubs Lane. This enormous graveyard, covering an area of 56 acres (23 hectares), was opened in 1833. The cemetery has a gate on to the canal that was used for taking away surplus soil dug from graves. It is likely that it was also used for funerals that included a final voyage. Among the many celebrated people buried here are the engineer Isambard Kingdom Brunel and the writers Anthony Trollope, William Makepeace Thackeray and Wilkie Collins. This is also the last resting place of Charles Blondin, the tightrope walker. The cemetery has many trees and bushes, providing a welcome sanctuary for birds and other wildlife. There is a peaceful atmosphere here that can be experienced again at further parts of the canal.

The Great Western Railway runs parallel to the canal to the Scrubs Lane Bridge (Bridge 6) and then veers away until the far end of the Paddington Canal. Standing on the bridge and looking southwards over the former railway marshalling yards of Old Oak Common, you can see the wide expanse of Wormwood Scrubs with the famous prison and Hammersmith Hospital in the background. The marshalling yards and the old engine sheds are replaced by the facilities used by modern trains including the new Elizabeth line. The open grassy space of Wormwood Scrubs was used by pioneer aviators at the beginning of the 20th century. Tucked into the north-west corner between the bridge and the canal is a small garden, a memorial to Mary Seacourt, the Jamaican-born nurse who cared for British soldiers in the Crimean War.

In Willesden, two railway bridges cross the canal. Between them, on the offside of the canal, lies Old Oak Wharf, which has a new life as a waste management centre with the potential of receiving barges carrying waste. From Old Oak Lane Bridge (Bridge 7) there is a short walk northwards to The Fishermans Arms pub and Willesden Junction station (*Underground – Bakerloo line; London Overground to Euston*). On the south (towpath) side, there is a café in the glass-faced building with a terrace overlooking the canal.

WILLESDEN TO HORSENDEN (3 miles, 5km)

After passing an industrial area under development for Park Royal, and a high railway bridge, you will come to Acton Power Station, which got its coal supplies via the canal. Water from the canal is still used in the power station's cooling system.

At Acton Lane Bridge (Bridge 7), the Grand Junction Arms pub has a waterside frontage with a garden and moorings for visiting boats and there is a restaurant on the towpath side. Harlesden station (*Underground – Bakerloo line; London Overground to Euston*) and the Central Middlesex Hospital are nearby. On the offside of the canal, a stream enters from Brent Reservoir (Welsh Harp), which was built to supply water for the Paddington and Grand Union Canals.

Park Royal is the large industrial area on both sides of the canal. Its name is derived from the site of the Royal Agricultural Society's annual shows, but this venture ended in 1903. It had large munitions factories in the First World War. In 1923, Park Royal Estate had 73 factories employing 13,400 people. Then came famous companies, such as Guinness and Heinz, which used the canal extensively to bring in raw materials and to distribute their products. In modern times, it has 1200 business and 35,000 workers, and occupies 500 hectares (1200 acres). Of these, a high proportion are 'hi-tech' and see the canal as a leisure amenity and not a means of transport.

The North Circular Aqueduct is obvious to the canal user, giving boaters and walkers a view of the traffic jams below. It is often unnoticed by the motorists beneath them. Perhaps that is just as well as it would be disastrous if it sprang a leak! The first aqueduct here was built in 1830, to be replaced by a bigger one to cross the North Circular Road in 1933. That was partly damaged by an IRA bomb in 1939. It was extended and rebuilt with two channels when the North Circular was widened in 1993. The coat of arms from the 1933 structure remain between the two channels. This place is also known as Stonebridge Park, after the ancient crossing over the River Brent that flows under the canal.

Beyond the North Circular, there are many new apartment blocks, most with some style of 'waterside living'. The canal becomes more peaceful with homes and light industry on its banks. Here you may meet some of the wonderful volunteers,

Crossing the North Circular Aqueduct.

Alperton.

The Friends of the Grand Union, who regularly pick litter. At Alperton, an old wharf on the offside was once the local council's rubbish disposal point. Refuse boats worked down the canal from Paddington collecting rubbish from various locations. They went in convoy to tips at West Drayton and Cowley to be loaded with sand and gravel to bring back to building sites in central London. There is another branch of Sainsbury's supermarket near Ealing Road Bridge. Alperton station (*Underground – Piccadilly line*) is over the bridge. The underside of the bridge has cheerful paintings, including one that looks like the corner of a sitting room, complete with settee, table lamp and cat!

As anticipated by the bridge paintings, the canal now takes on a suburban air, with views into back gardens, willow trees and glimpses of Sunbury golf course. After Manor Farm Road at Piggery Bridge (Bridge 12), the landscape becomes rural. The canal widens, flowers from gardens spill over the towpath, and the trees on Horsenden Hill appear on the offside. A traditional humpback bridge leads into the moorings of the West London Motor Cruising Club, which has a full range of facilities for visiting boats.

Soon you come to Ballot Box Bridge (Bridge 13), which gets its name from a pub (long gone) that was used as a polling station for boatmen. The finger post shows that this is 7¼ miles (11.6km) from Paddington and 5¾ miles (9.2km) from Bulls Bridge. Note the tie-beams on the bridge have the canal company's initials and the year 1909. This must be a favourite part of the canal for West Londoners, who can park at Horsenden Farm Visitor Centre, come by underground to Perivale station (*Underground – Central line, ¼ mile (0.5km) along Horsenden Lane*), or walk via the Capital Ring Path. Energetic walkers can take a diversion to see the fine views from the summit of Horsenden Hill.

A WALK UP HORSENDEN HILL
(*1 mile/1.5km there and back*)

Leave the canal and cross Ballot Box Bridge. Turn into the Visitors Centre where there is parking space, a café (open at weekends, 11am–2pm), picnic tables, a shop, a volunteer centre, a rock garden and a play area. The first part of the path up the hill is marked as the Gruffalo Trail and goes past the Ealing Canoe Club. Go through the gate out of the Visitor Centre (locked at night) and straight up the hill to the woodland, unless you want to follow the Gruffalo Trail, which turns off to the right. Continue through the trees to the top where there are superlative views of west London.

HORSENDEN TO BULLS BRIDGE (5¾ miles, 9km)

Continuing towards Northolt, the rural landscape proceeds with a meadow and Perivale Wood on the towpath side. Perivale Wood is an oak wood with a carpet of bluebells in the spring. It is one of the oldest nature reserves in Britain and is owned by the Selbourne Society, which promotes learning about conservation. Entry is restricted to members of the Society and to school and youth groups by arrangement. The leaf of the oak tree is a symbol of the London Borough of Ealing, which has a very active open-space and countryside department.

An attractive wooden footbridge (Bridge 15b) gives you an alternative route to Horsenden Hill across wide open fields often ablaze with buttercups in the springtime. Another diversion can be taken to Paradise Fields on the towpath side. This is a scrub and wetland nature reserve with a viewing platform at the main pond, and paths that lead to Westway shopping centre.

The scene changes dramatically as you go under Greenford Road Bridge (Bridge 15a). A tall block of flats and offices stands on Greenford Quay, with new developments on all sides.

The Black Horse pub at Oldfield Road gives its name to Bridge 15, from where it is a short walk to Greenford station (*National Rail to Paddington; Underground – Central line*). The pub has a canalside garden and a mooring for visitors.

Soon after, the towpath rises over the entrance to Lyons Dock. Here the famous food business had extensive warehouses and factories making cakes and supplying the chain of Lyons' Corner Houses all over London. Lyons was the last private dock to be built in London, in 1922. Tea was imported through the London Docks and coal came from the Midlands to fuel the ovens and steam plants. Soon after its construction, the dock received a royal visit by King George V and Queen Mary, who came to inspect the new mechanical equipment used to unload the barges. At the time the factory had the largest tea-packing plant in the world.

Paddington Arm sign at Greenford.

A WALK TO ST MARY'S CHURCH, NORTHOLT
(⅔ mile/1km there and back)

If you have time, it is worth walking over the iron footbridge (Bridge 16a) to St Mary's Church, Northolt, which is visible on a small hill ¼ mile (0.5km) away. The way is along a short footpath to Rowdell Road and up the grass path in Belvue Park. The white walled church and its distinctive spire was built in the 13th century, but there has been a village here since Saxon times. Beyond the church is the centre of Northholt village, with its green overlooked by a pub, a stream and a village hall nearby. St Mary's Church and its surroundings are part of the Northolt and Greenford Countryside Park. This extends beyond the A40 Western Avenue and is bisected by the canal. It incorporates parkland, a golf course, playing fields and scrubland that was once brickfields – a huge green space of 270 acres (109 hectares) that exemplifies Ealing's commitment to conservation. Northolt station (*Underground – Central line*) can be reached along Ealing Road and Mandeville Road, ¼ mile (0.5km) from the village centre.

The new developments at Greenford Quay.

In 1926, the company expanded its site to the opposite side of the canal, where a new factory called Bridge Park began making ice cream. The ice-cream business was sold in 1992 and the main factory was demolished ten years later. All of this has been replaced by modern light industry and warehouses, mostly hidden by the trees beside the towpath.

Lines of residential moorings begin after the railway bridge that carries the Central line trains of the London Underground.

The moorings are managed by the High Line Yachting boatyard situated at the next footbridge. Before the footbridge, the beautiful walls and minarets of Northolt Mosque rise above the trees on the canal offside bank.

The towpath goes under the A40 Western Avenue at Bridge 17b. Beside the towpath lies Marnham Fields, a wooded nature reserve created from disused brickfields. Then the canal reaches a pleasant residential area in Ruislip. Taylor Woodrow, the former

Willowtree Marina, Paddington Canal.

engineering firm had its headquarters at Ruislip Road Bridge (Bridge 18), as commemorated by a brick mosaic of its logo beside the towpath. The offices have been replaced by a housing project called Grand Union Village in keeping with the canal at its heart shown by a new set of moorings at the Engineers Wharf.

From here on, the canal is heading southwards toward Bulls Bridge, 3 miles (5km) away, with no more twists and turns. A row of stately poplar trees on the offside mark the start of a fine piece of landscaped parkland, the Willow Tree Open Space. A handsome

suspension bridge carries the Hillingdon Trail to join the towpath down the Grand Union main line. The entrance to Willowtree Marina is just beyond the bridge. This attractive marina has two large basins for boat moorings, formed from excavations in the Hayes brickfields. It has facilities for visitors and resident boats, plus a restaurant and wine bar.

Three substantial arms led into the brickfields. Later, when the fields were worked out, the rubbish boats from Paddington used the docks. One of the arms, Yeading Dock, had incinerators for burning rubbish. In the end, it could not cope with the vast amounts coming in by boat, so the rubbish was buried in the ground.

Spikes Bridge (Bridge 19) links housing estates on either side of the canal. The Hillingdon Trail and the Dog Rose Ramble can be followed from Spikes Bridge into Yeading Valley Park, which makes a green corridor towards Hillingdon and Uxbridge. Yeading Brook, which flows down this corridor and then parallel to the canal, will become the River Crane near Bulls Bridge. Offside moorings are followed by modern housing and a huge storage building. On the towpath side, there is an Army Reserve Centre, formerly the Territorial Army barracks. A strange octagonal tower looking like a lighthouse by the Uxbridge Road catches the eye as you approach Hayes Bridge (Bridge 20) in Southall. There are shops and a wide choice of Indian restaurants, reflecting the large Asian community. Buses go to Uxbridge in one direction and to Ealing in the other. To reach Southall station (*National Rail to Paddington*), turn left along the Broadway; at the town hall, turn right along South Road.

The final mile of the canal is wider, possibly because there were wharves in the past. Trees overhang the water and there are few residential boats alongside, so it feels more spacious. On the east (towpath) side, the former Southall gasworks has become a large building site with 3750 homes planned, called the Green Quarter. Once there was a series of arms, one of which served Kearley and Tonge's jam factory. The journey from coal mines at Atherstone to the factory was known as the 'Jam 'ole run' and has been re-enacted using one of the original working narrowboats, the *Raymond*. On the offside lies Minet Country Park with a large sports ground and a nature reserve. Finally, you go under a new road bridge (Bridge 21a) into the Green Quarter, then under an old friend, the Great Western Railway, on Bridge 21b. Ahead is the welcome sight of the stone arch of Bulls Bridge. The wharf next to the bridge is still working, loading building materials to be carried by barge. It is heartening to see that the canal still has a commercial function.

A misty view of Bulls Bridge.

To reach Hayes & Harlington station (National Rail to Paddington and Reading), turn right at Bulls Bridge and walk beside the Grand Union main line canal for ½ mile (1km) to Bridge 200 (Station Road). Turn left on Station Road. The station is just after the row of shops.

The Regent's Canal

8½ miles (13.5km) with 12 locks

Canal highlights

- Little Venice
- Lisson Grove
- Regent's Park
- London Zoo
- Camden Lock
- King's Cross Centre with St Pancras Basin
- London Canal Museum
- Victoria Park
- Hertford Union Canal
- Limehouse Basin

Canalside mansions in Regent's Park.

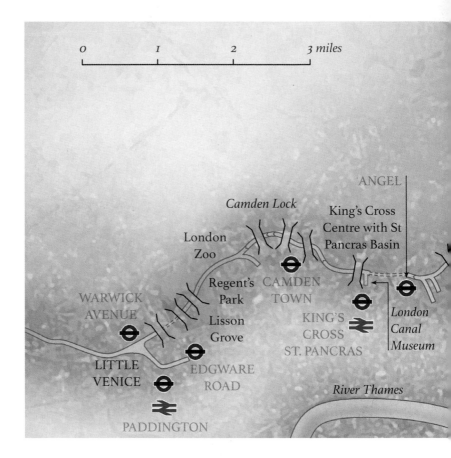

HISTORY

In 1802, a commercial speculator named Thomas Homer, who already had canal interests, had the idea to drive a canal from London Docks to the centre of London. Even in those days the cost of land in central London was prohibitive so Homer looked towards Marylebone Park on the northern outskirts of the city, where the architect John Nash was building what would become Regent's Park. Homer consulted Nash and suggested that the proposed canal should run through his park. Nash was enthusiastic and subsequently became the driving force in the construction of the new canal. An Act of Parliament was passed

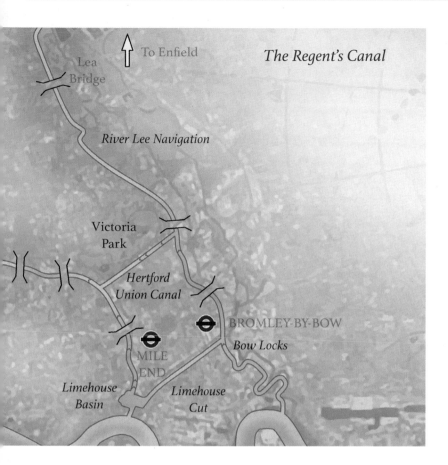

in 1812 for a canal from the Thames at Limehouse to Paddington, thereby linking up with the Grand Junction Canal as it was then called. The Prince Regent, later George IV, had consented to the new park being named after him, and so the canal eventually took his title too. The canal bridges are adorned with the three feathers emblem of the prince, who was also the Prince of Wales.

Nash wanted the canal to go through the centre of the park, but the Crown Commissioners objected. They thought that working boats and their crews would lower the tone of such a fashionable place of recreation. Therefore, the canal was banished to a cutting in the northern edge of the park. It was soon beset by more problems. An intransigent landowner, William Agar, objected to the canal and forcibly defended his property against the navvies. The engineer James Morgan, who was put in charge by Nash, had no canal experience and made mistakes in several places, including the tunnels. To make things worse, Thomas Homer embezzled most of the company's funds. He was eventually arrested, tried and transported. The failure of a new design of lock, the hydropneumatic lock, invented by William Congreve, necessitated the rebuilding of Hampstead Road Lock in 1819. Congreve (later Sir William) became famous for military rockets and rolling ball clocks.

Despite the difficulties, the canal from Paddington to Camden was opened in 1816 and the full 8½ miles (13.5km) to Limehouse completed in 1820. It is a wide canal, built for heavily laden barges, and has two tunnels. The canal opened too late to be a complete financial success as railway competition was soon felt. In 1845 a consortium was founded to convert the canal into a railway but financial constraints and opposition from the Grand Junction Canal Company stopped that scheme. The Grand Junction's opposition is an indication of the rivalry between Limehouse and Brentford in the transhipment of goods between sea-going vessels and canal boats.

LITTLE VENICE TO KING'S CROSS (3½ miles, 5.5km)

The Regent's Canal begins at Little Venice (see page 63) (*nearest station Warwick Avenue: Underground – Bakerloo line*). If walking from Paddington station and Basin, cross the blue painted iron lattice bridge to the north side of the triangular Little Venice pool to where Jason's Trip boats are moored. *Jason* is a boat that is more than 100 years old and was the first public canal boat in modern times, starting in 1951. On the path, look down for the Jubilee Greenway pavement sign that can guide you all the way to Limehouse. The Jubilee Greenway was designed by Transport for London (TfL) to mark the Diamond Jubilee of Queen Elizabeth II in 2012. It is a walking and cycling route that links Buckingham Palace to the 2012 Olympic site. Sections 2, 3 and 10 are on the Regent's Canal towpath and a website has detailed maps and information. It is a tribute to the excellence of the Regent's Canal that three out of ten parts of the Jubilee Greenway are on this towpath. Walking from Jason's Trip boats along the towpath, you pass more trip boats near Warwick Avenue Junction Bridge. On the left is Junction House, which was the tollhouse for the Regent's Canal. Lines of colourful moored boats lead the canal to Maida Vale. The boatowners have a locked gate on the towpath, so you must walk along the pavement of Blomfield Road.

Maida Vale tunnel lies at the end of Blomfield Road. The tunnel, 272 yards (249m) long, has no towpath. Before the days of engine power, the crew 'legged' their boat through the tunnel by lying on their backs on planks and driving the boat with their legs, using their feet to 'walk' along the tunnel wall. Meanwhile, the horse walked over the hill above the tunnel. A café above the

Jubilee Greenway sign.

A Regent's Canal sign.

entrance to the tunnel has wonderful views of the boats passing below. This might have been the site of the Lord's Cricket Ground if the canal had not been built on the land that Thomas Lord had originally intended for the Marylebone Cricket Club (MCC). Compensation was paid and Lord built his cricket ground at St John's Wood, using soil excavated from the canal.

Walkers must follow the path of the boat horses, crossing the busy Maida Vale into Aberdeen Place. At the end of the road, opposite an ornate building called 'Crockers Folly', you will see a gap in the wall and a steep ramp down to the towpath. For nearly a century, Crockers Folly was a pub called The Crown. It acquired the nickname because the original owner, Frank Crocker, thought that the Grand Central Railway would have its terminus nearby and so furnished his pub to be a grand station hotel. It was said that Crocker was so disappointed when the railway station was built at Marylebone that he committed suicide by jumping out of an upper window, and his ghost haunted the pub. In fact, Crocker

Decorative wrought ironwork at Lisson Grove.

died by natural causes, but who would let the truth spoil a good story? Now the building has a restaurant on the ground floor and flats on the higher floors.

Walking on the towpath on the north side of the canal to Lisson Grove, you will notice an attractive modern riverside garden on the opposite bank where the Westminster Adult Learning Centre is based. At Lisson Grove, walk up to and across the road, then turn right to the south side of the canal and then left through a decorative gate into Lisson Green. The wrought ironwork above the gate depicts animals, insects, a canal boat and even a bottle of wine and a boot. The housing estate was built on the old Marylebone railway goods yard. The colourful canal boats moored the other side of the canal have little gardens on the bank. At the end of the housing estate, the way crosses the canal on a green painted footbridge to rejoin what was the original towpath. Pass under two rather gloomy railway bridges and Park Road Bridge (Bridge 7) to enter Regent's Park.

Moorings at Lisson Grove.

Macclesfield Bridge,
aka Blow-up Bridge.

In Regent's Park, the canal is at first flanked by handsome mansions with well-maintained gardens sweeping down to the water. It continues along a wooded cutting that is parallel to Prince Albert Road. It looks particularly lovely in October and November when the mature trees display their autumn colours. This is one of the finest urban stretches of waterway anywhere in Britain.

The first bridge (Bridge 8) carries a path from Prince Albert Road to the boating lake. The second, with five iron columns on each side, is the celebrated Macclesfield Bridge known as 'Blow-up Bridge'. Here, in the early hours of 2 October 1874, the barge *Tilbury*, carrying five tons of gunpowder, exploded with devastating results. All that remained of the bridge was a pile of bricks 10 feet (3m) high above the water. Nothing was found of the crew of three. Nearby houses were damaged and windows shattered. The effect on the animals at London Zoo was not

Regent's Park – the finest
stretch of canal in Britain.

officially recorded but it is said that extra wheelbarrows had to be brought into the elephant house!

When the bridge was rebuilt, the original columns were saved and re-used. The columns were replaced in reverse, so that the old towing-rope grooves were on the outer sides, away from the canal. The columns now have grooves on both sides – one set worn before 1874 and the other set afterwards. The word 'Coalbrookdale' at the top of the columns refers to the town on the River Severn in Shropshire where the columns were made.

After another fine iron bridge (Bridge 10), the canal enters the London Zoo. The magnificent Snowdon Aviary dominates the scene; the iconic structure was restored in 2021 to become the new home for a troop of colobus monkeys and renamed 'Monkey Valley'. If you are walking on the towpath, you will have to go to the far end of the zoo and cross on Bridge 13, which takes you to

London Zoo with the Snowdon Aviary before its recent renovation.

the zoo entrance. If you are coming by boat from Little Venice, you will arrive in style at the Zoo Pier, with its elegant little shelter. In summer, this section of the canal is busy with trip boats and water buses, and the towpath is filled with walkers, joggers and office workers enjoying a lunchtime break.

The first architect for the Zoological Society of London, to use its full title, was Decimus Burton who also designed Marble Arch. The zoo opened to the public in 1828 and it has thousands of animals in its 36 acres (15 hectares). Most of the visitors are unaware of the important research that has been the primary

Jason's trip boat near Camden.

purpose of the zoo since its foundation, but their entry fees and donations are vital to its upkeep.

After the zoo, the canal turns left to Camden Town. At the turn, the Cumberland Basin is filled with a bright-red floating Chinese restaurant towering over a pack of moored narrow boats. A canal arm once ran for ½ mile (1km) to Cumberland Hay Market near Euston station. It was filled after the Second World War and partly covered by the zoo's car park.

An immediate change of scene follows the canal's change of direction. The greenery of Regent's Park gives way to tall houses with colourful gardens visible through a tangle of willow trees. Look out for a pair of horse ramps that are close to the path. At the next bridge (Bridge 16), there are steps up to Gloucester Avenue. In the days of steam, there would have been a pall of smoke from nearby Euston station. Trains leaving the station faced a steep incline to cross the Regent's Canal and originally had to be assisted by cable haulage.

Trip boat *Perseus* near Camden Lock.

The next road bridge (Bridge 20a) is one of the strangest sights on the canal: The Pirate Castle boating centre. The medieval appearance is deceptive (very piratical) as the walls were built in 1977. Founded as a youth club, it has evolved into a vibrant community centre providing canoeing, boat trips and other watersports for people of all ages and abilities. Go under the battlements and you see Camden Lock ahead. First the towpath climbs over a tunnel into a large warehouse on your left (north) side. This arm of the canal was a canal-to-railway interchange. Being enclosed, it was secure enough for wines and spirits to be loaded. It was known by some locals as the 'Camden Catacombs' and by others as 'Dead Dog Tunnel'.

An elegant roving bridge that carries the towpath to the opposite bank frames the double Hampstead Road Locks, commonly called 'Camden Lock'. This pair of locks brings an

A busy day at Camden Lock, Regent's Canal.

end to 27 miles (43km) of the lock-free pound from Cowley on the Grand Union main line. From the top of the bridge, you have a good view of one of the liveliest markets in Britain. Camden Lock Centre opened in 1973 around a complex of old canal buildings that included a timber yard and stables. The large winch beneath the roving bridge was moved from a disused lock at Limehouse. Another symbol of old canal times is the statue of a man lifting an ice block on Ice Wharf. Today the market has a huge variety of goods, ranging from pianos to spices. The shops, cafés, galleries and street stalls spread into the surrounding streets, making Camden Lock a popular tourist destination. The TE Dingwall Building is a well-known centre for comedy and music. The white castellated lock keeper's cottage was turned into an information centre but has become a coffee house with a pub and hotel next door. The London Waterbus Company's boats are moored at the

Angel at Camden Lock.

canal's arm in the market, and the *Jenny Wren* boats are based at Walker's Wharf just below Chalk Farm Bridge. These trip boats have a regular service to Little Venice. *The nearest station is Camden Town (Underground – Northern line).*

Hampstead Road Locks are the only pair of locks that are still in regular use. The rest have been reduced to singles with the second chamber blocked off or cascaded, thus saving water and maintenance. The towpath continues down a ramp from the lock under the iron bridge (Bridge 24) bearing Chalk Farm Road. The emblem of three white feathers looks handsome on the black background of the bridge. The canal winds between high office buildings and a set of pod-like apartments. Down at water level, there are horse ramps at intervals. Some boatmen used the ramps to wash their horses, much to the annoyance of the canal company.

The next section passes through the once notorious Agar's Town, named after the landlord William Agar, who objected to the canal being built across his land (see pages 69–70). Agar's town was so squalid and crowded that it was nicknamed 'Ague Town'. The building of the Midland Railway and St Pancras station cleared most of the slums, and today the canalside properties are charming. The railway passes over the canal on a tunnel-like bridge. Beyond the bridge, the canal opens out, revealing the stunning new development around former gasholders. These striking flats and offices have wonderful views of St Pancras Basin, its lock and the St Pancras Cruising Club. Originally the basin was a coal wharf for the Midland Railway Company. Beyond the lock on the offside of the canal is Camley Street Natural Park, which was opened in 1984 and was the first artificially created park to be designated as a local nature reserve. The Natural Park, managed by the London Wildlife Trust and only 2 acres (1 hectare) in size, has a café and is well worth the diversion across the footbridge below the lock.

On the towpath side lies the very modern King's Cross Centre. Here are shops, restaurants and stages for music and drama, with lots of space to sit and chat. Climb some steps and you can stroll

King's Cross.

along a former railway viaduct, Bagley Walk, looking down on the canal on one side and into Coal Drops Yard on the other. Coal trucks used to drop their loads from this viaduct to the arched spaces below. Now there is a lively scene that can be compared with Camden Market. The Regent's Canal is as fashionable as its name suggests. Amid all this modernity, it is heartening to see canal boats still being used to convey construction materials and waste.

The canal turns sharply to the left to where a flight of steps leads up to the Coal Drops Yard. After a new concrete bridge, it widens where the railway lines from King's Cross station pass through tunnels under the canal. The next bridge, Maiden Road Bridge (Bridge 35), was built in 1819 and has been rebuilt three times since. In the Second World War, gates were installed by it as a precaution to prevent the canal flooding the railway tunnel if it were bombed. The road that it carries is now called York Way. *Turn right on the bridge for King's Cross stations (National Rail; Underground – Circle, Hammersmith & City, Metropolitan, Northern, Piccadilly and Victoria lines).*

St Pancras Lock.

KING'S CROSS TO LIMEHOUSE (5 miles, 8km)

After the bridge, Battlebridge Basin comes into view. This is the home of the London Canal Museum, housed in a former ice-cream warehouse built in the 1850s by Carlo Gatti. Blocks of ice were imported from Norway and carried from Limehouse in canal boats. Ice wells beneath the warehouse have been excavated and are on view to the public. This together with the Ice Wharf at Camden are reminders of what must have been part of an extensive trade to serve the grand houses in London in Victorian times. The museum tells the story of the development of London's canals and the people who worked the boats in its heyday. Among the wharves and yards around the basin were the warehouses used by John Dickinson's paper mills which were on the River Gade (part of the Grand Union) near Hemel Hempstead in Hertfordshire. Boats brought paper from the mills and reloaded with wood pulp and rags for the return journey. Battlebridge is an old name for King's Cross and the basin has moorings for canal boats, including those restored by the museum. As the basin is on the opposite side to the towpath, visitors to the museum should turn right over the next bridge (Caledonian Road), right into All Saints Road and left at the end in New Wharf Road.

Back at the towpath, the gaping mouth of Islington Tunnel ends this section of the canalside walk. The tunnel is 960 yards (878 metres) long and has no towpath. As at Maida Vale, boats had to be 'legged' through this tunnel (see page 71) until 1826, when they were pulled through by a steam tug. The tug had a steam engine that powered a winch that pulled the tug and the towed boats along a chain fixed at both ends of the tunnel.

It is possible to see light at the other end of the tunnel, which is a sign of excellent surveying and engineering. Some older tunnels elsewhere in Britain had kinks and curves that make it impossible to see light until more than halfway through.

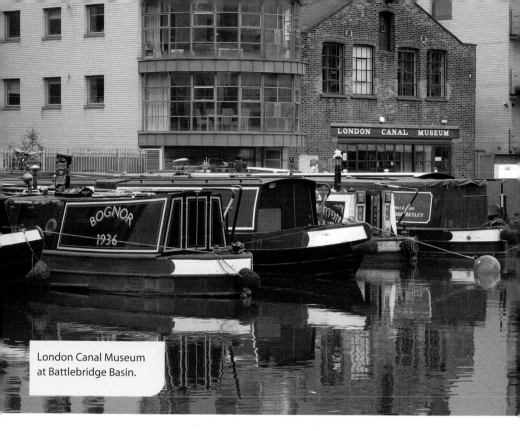

London Canal Museum
at Battlebridge Basin.

Walkers today follow the way taken by the boat horses over the top, often in the charge of the boatmen's children. Look for watery symbols on the pavement that mark the trail. At the top of the tunnel, cross the road and join a path that leads between the flats. Pass a school and turn right into Barnsbury Road. Cross the road in front of a church to Chapel Market. At the far end of Chapel Market, turn right. At the T-junction with Upper Street, cross over to the other side near Angel station (*Underground – Northern line*). Turn left away from the station and pass The York pub. Turn right into Duncan Street and walk to the end. A gap in the railings brings you down to the eastern portal of the Islington Tunnel.

The Islington Tunnel opens out into a tree-lined cutting flanked by smart terraced houses with well-kept gardens. Weeping willows and an old brick warehouse on the offside frame a view of the City Road Lock, with a modern apartment block in the middle ground and the City of London skyscrapers in the distance.

Regent's Canal near City Road Lock.

City Road Basin.

City Road Basin lies below the lock. In the early days of the canal, Pickfords Carriers had 120 boats and 400 horses working out of the basin. When Pickfords moved elsewhere, it was replaced by the renowned canal carriers Fellows, Morton & Clayton. Now the land around the basin is being developed with apartments and offices, and the water is used for watersports. It is the home of Islington Boat Club, which has an active programme for people of all ages, including courses on powerboating, kayaking and canoeing.

Wenlock Basin.

Wenlock Basin lies a short distance to the east of City Road. It has been privately owned since it was started in 1825. It opened by accident in 1826 when the dam across its mouth collapsed, draining so much water from the canal that the level fell by 13 inches (33cm). It is now a private marina for residential boats, surrounded by trees and equipped with full facilities – rather a contrast to some of the boats moored along the towpath. The Narrowboat pub at Wharf Road Bridge (Bridge 39) is opposite the Wenlock Basin. The towpath has been pleasantly landscaped, with seating for walkers. If you look up, you will see that some of the office and apartment blocks have gardens on their roofs.

Passing Sturt's Lock and Bridge 42, you will notice on the offside a building with the sign 'Rosemary Works'. Although the words conjure up an image of warehouses full of herbs, it is in fact a school, skilfully redesigned from a block of flats named after the nearby Rosemary Gardens. After Whitmore Bridge (Bridge 43), there is the Towpath Café and other food outlets. A café combined with community office space is on the edge of a short arm, formerly called Kingsland Basin. This is now Reliance Wharf, a pleasant small marina. The renovation and rebuilding of old canalside buildings has made a big difference. The quirky shape and colour of Laburnum Boat Club and the mosaics made by schoolchildren at Laburnum Bridge should bring a smile to towpath travellers.

In the 19th century, Acton's Lock was described as a lawless area. The buildings are still rather sombre. Grilles on doors and windows show that present-day residents must be security conscious. An old gasometer looms over Mare Street Bridge, perhaps the last one by London's canals. Redevelopment is happening, but as you can see here and further east towards Limehouse and the Lee Navigation, there is still work to be done. *Cambridge Heath station (London Overground to Liverpool Street) is nearby.*

Soon the green oasis of Victoria Park comes into view. Created by an Act of Parliament in 1841, the park opened in 1848 and is by far the largest open space in London's East End. It was the first park in London to be made specifically for local people, for them to be able to walk and play outside their crowded tenements. Unsurprisingly it has been the setting for political rallies as well as for daily walks and weekend games. It has a large lake that is studded with islands bright with rhododendrons in springtime. A wild deer park in East London comes as something of a surprise but there are also more conventional facilities such as a café and playing fields. You may notice a Jubilee Greenway sign on the pavement at the towpath entrance to the park. This is because one arm of the Greenway goes through the park and over to the Olympic Park beside the River Lea. The other arm continues down the Regent's Canal to Limehouse.

Old Ford Lock has a more rural atmosphere than most others along this canal. The stables by the lock would have provided fresh horses to pull the laden boats coming from Limehouse. The lock keeper's cottage and the stables are both listed buildings. Soon after the lock the towpath rises over the entrance to the Hertford Union Canal.

The Hertford Union Canal is 1½ miles (2.5km) long and has three locks. It is also known as Duckett's canal, after Sir George Duckett, whose father had been involved with the Stort Navigation, a canal that linked Bishop's Stortford to the Lee Navigation. The Hertford Union opened in 1830 and provided a short cut to the Lee Navigation avoiding the 5 mile (8km) journey down to Limehouse and through the Limehouse Cut. It was not a commercial success and it was put up for sale in 1851. It was bought by the Regent's Canal Company in 1857 and a trade developed, with imported timber going to furniture factories on the Lee Navigation. It remains in good condition today as an avenue for leisure craft to explore the borders between London, Essex and Hertfordshire. Some years ago there was a plan to keep large tanks of live eels in the canal to cater for the East End market for jellied eels, but permission was refused. Walking from the Regent's Canal towards the Lee, there is a pretty terrace of houses on the towpath side and then the pleasant ambience of Victoria Park for most of the way. On the offside, Bow Wharf has smart flats, moorings, a café, a bar and boutique shops.

Further along on the offside is a large new development of apartments called Fish Island Village. The lock here is not nearly as deep as the first two, and its purpose was to adjust for variation in the water levels of the Lee Navigation.

Back to the Regent's Canal, it is nearly 2 miles (3km) to Limehouse. The theme of large modern apartment blocks on the offside and parks on the towpath side continues down to the Mile End Road. The parks are Wennington Green, an ecology park with reedbeds and ponds, and Mile End Park with sports grounds. Canary Wharf and neighbouring skyscrapers appear in the distance as you come close to Mile End Lock. *To reach Mile End station (Underground – Central and District lines), climb the steps at Mile End Bridge and turn left.*

Near Johnson's Lock, the Ragged School Museum spreads over three Victorian warehouses. It was once a free school set up by Dr Barnardo's for the children of poor families. It is now a museum of East End life run by volunteers, and has a towpath café and shop. Beyond the Mile End Stadium, a lonely chimney stands by the towpath, but the factory that it served has long gone and a grass field remains. A ramp and footbridge have brightened up the environs of Salmon Lane Lock. Factories and offices rear up on both sides at Commercial Road Lock. Here, only the canal is no longer commercial.

And so you come to Limehouse Basin, formerly called Regent's Canal Dock, built in 1820. Produce and raw materials from all over the world were loaded onto canal boats for distribution throughout England. The dock also exported all manner of produce and remained active until the late 1960s. Over the years it was enlarged five times: 2.25 million tons of coal were unloaded in 1876. The old Limehouse Locks leading to the Thames were closed in 1968 and a new section of canal was built to connect Limehouse Cut to the dock. A broad tidal lock was constructed, with direct access to the dock, but all this enthusiasm was short-lived as the dock was closed to shipping by 1970. Commercial activity ended and gave way to recreational use. The cranes stood collecting rust and an air of dereliction prevailed for many years. What you see now is an amazing transformation, with the old dock surrounded by modern housing in keeping with the development of the rest of Docklands. The water space has become Limehouse Marina, filled with a variety of canal, river and sea-going craft.

The Cruising Association has its headquarters opposite an octagonal cabin that controls the tidal lock. The Hydraulic Accumulator Tower is one of the few old buildings still surviving in the dock. It was part of a pumping station built in 1869 that had

Limehouse Marina at Limehouse Basin.

its engine and boilers beneath the railway arches that now carry the Docklands Light Railway (DLR). The tower is sometimes open for visits and gives you wonderful views over the docks. Down at ground level, you will see one of the Jubilee Greenway signs that have led you all the way here.

Limehouse station (National Rail to Fenchurch Street; DLR) is in the north-east corner of the dock.

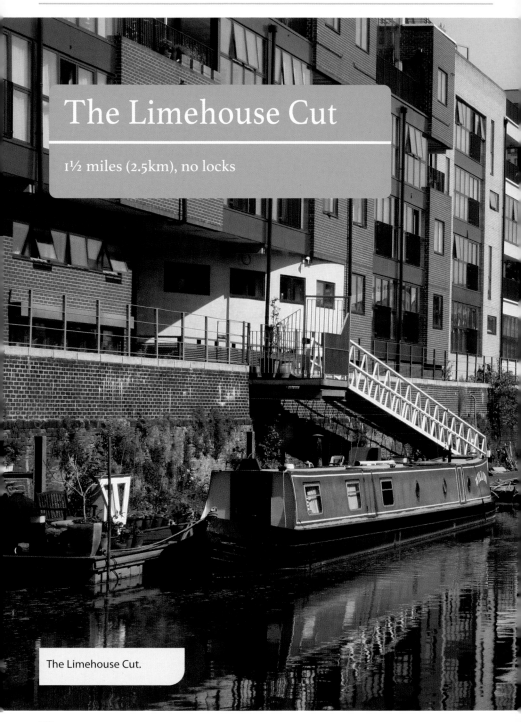

The Limehouse Cut

1½ miles (2.5km), no locks

The Limehouse Cut.

Canal highlights

- St Anne's Church
- Bartlett Park

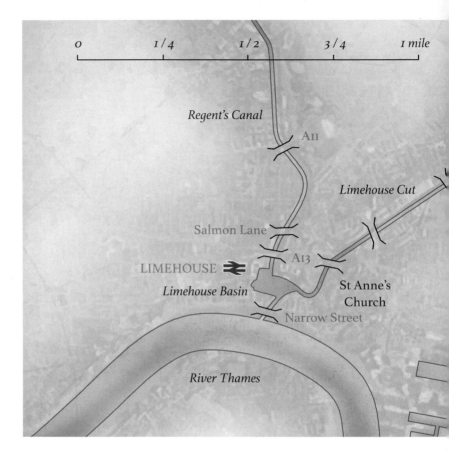

HISTORY

The Limehouse Cut was built in 1770 and widened in 1777, at about the time when the pound locks were being built on the Lee Navigation. It connects the River Lee Navigation at Bow Locks to Limehouse Basin and the Thames, avoiding the winding loops of Bow Creek. It is a wide, straight canal that passes through an intensely built-up area. It was once shut away from public access but the towpath has been much improved in the last 20 years. It is now a pleasant addition to the walks along London's canals. Indeed, it can form one side of a 6-mile (9.5km) walk that goes from Limehouse to Bow Locks, beside the Lee Navigation to

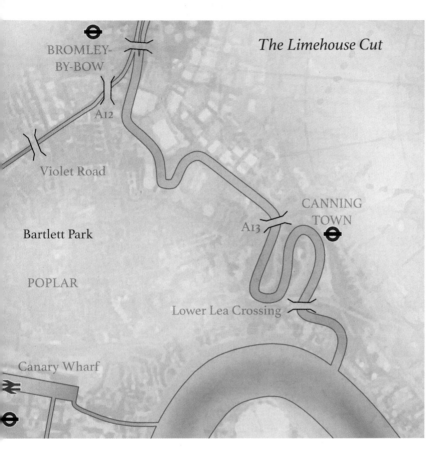

Sweet Water (see page 110), along the Hertford Union (see page 95) to the Regent's, and back down Limehouse.

LIMEHOUSE TO BOW LOCKS   (1½ miles, 2km)

From the Commercial Lock, the last lock on the Regent's Canal, look for the signpost showing the way to the Limehouse Cut. You can either go behind the apartment block and pass the Hydraulic Accumulator Tower or go on the waterside path in front of the apartments. Both ways bring you to a footbridge over the Cut. The path takes a right-hand spiral down to the towpath along the Cut. On a sunny morning, the new residences on the offside have a light, spacious ambience in contrast to the darker towpath in the shade of a high brick wall. Immediately after going under the Docklands Light Railway (DLR) bridge at King's Wharf, you have a lovely view of St Anne's Church, designed by the revered English architect Nicholas Hawksmoor and consecrated in 1730. Being close to the Thames, it had a royal warrant for ships' captains to register important events at sea. Hence the church has the right to fly the White Ensign and its prominent tower is a 'sea-mark' on charts.

The pattern of new buildings on the offside and old buildings beside the towpath continues from Commercial Road bridge to Burdett Road where there is a local store close to the canal. Then there are modern buildings beside the towpath, nicely fitted around a small marina at Abbotts Wharf. Bartlett Park gives a green space and playground to local residents in the Lansbury Estate. The estate and park are a fitting tribute to George Lansbury (1859–1940), the local Labour politician who campaigned for public recreational spaces and other reforms that we now take for granted. Towards the Bow Locks end of the Cut, trees are beginning to colonise the canal banks, softening the appearance of new buildings. A floating walkway will take you under the Blackwall Tunnel Approach and bring you to Bow Locks near an office used by Thames21, whose band of volunteers have done much to clean up the waterways of London.

The Limehouse Cut.

The Lee Navigation

Bow to Waltham

12 miles (19km) with 9 locks (including Waltham Town)

Canal highlights

- Three Mills
- Old Ford Lock
- Sweetwater Trade Moorings
- Queen Elizabeth Olympic Park
- Middlesex Filter Beds
- Walthamstow Marsh Nature Reserve
- Markfield Beam Engine and Museum
- Lee Valley Reservoir Chain
- Enfield Island Village
- Waltham Abbey
- Royal Gunpowder Mills

Waltham Town Lock.

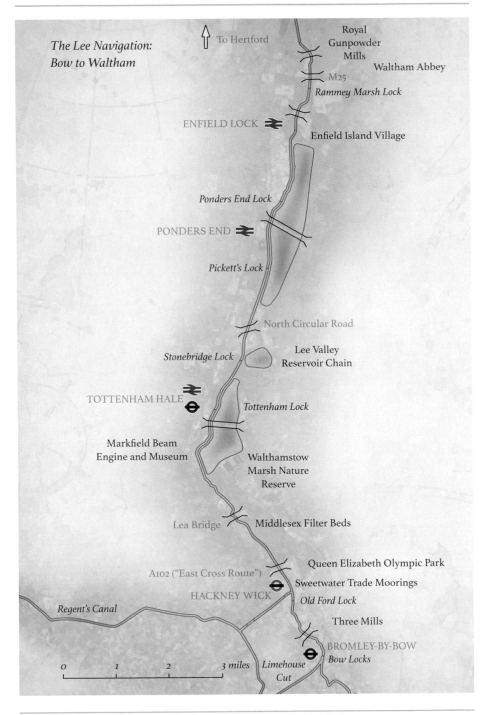

The Lee Navigation:
Bow to Waltham

↑ To Hertford

Royal
Gunpowder
Mills
Waltham Abbey

M25
Rammey Marsh Lock

ENFIELD LOCK

Enfield Island Village

Ponders End Lock

PONDERS END

Pickett's Lock

North Circular Road

Stonebridge Lock

Lee Valley
Reservoir Chain

TOTTENHAM HALE

Tottenham Lock

Markfield Beam
Engine and Museum

Walthamstow
Marsh Nature
Reserve

Lea Bridge

Middlesex Filter Beds

Queen Elizabeth Olympic Park

A102 ("East Cross Route")

Sweetwater Trade Moorings

HACKNEY WICK

Old Ford Lock

Three Mills

Regent's Canal

BROMLEY-BY-BOW
Bow Locks

0   1   2   3 miles   *Limehouse*
Cut

HISTORY

The Lee Navigation is based on the River Lea (both spellings are in common use) and forms a navigable waterway from Hertford to the Thames, with an arm up the River Stort to Bishop's Stortford. The River Lea was naturally navigable in Roman times and was used by the Danes to sail up to Hertford. The river was being used regularly to convey grain and flour from Ware to London in 1220. As on the non-tidal Thames above London, river trade was made more difficult by the building of weirs to power the water mills. The disputes between millers and bargemen were investigated by a series of commissions up to 1482. An Act of Parliament was passed in 1571 to create an artificial channel, a 'navigation', which was completed ten years later. Later the Lee had an additional function in providing drinking water for London, supplemented by the New River, which had been supplying spring water to London since 1613. Improvements to the navigation were made as the years progressed. Pound locks were introduced in 1779. New lock cuts were made in 1850. In the 1920s it was considerably enlarged so as to allow 130-ton barges through to Enfield and 100-ton craft to Ware. Increased traffic led to bottlenecks, and this was managed by mechanising the sluices and gates and by making double locks. Timber was an important cargo, initially from forests in Hertfordshire and Essex for building houses and ships, later imported wood for the furniture industry at Edmonton. Eventually the trade diminished, and regular freight traffic ended around 1984.

The Lee Valley Regional Park was established in 1966 and stretches for 26 miles (42km) along the banks of the River Lea. The park includes 10,000 acres (4,046 hectares) of recreational space. The Lee Valley Pathway was created in 1996, making a 28-mile (45km) pedestrian and cycle way from rural Hertfordshire to the River Thames.

BOW TO HACKNEY WICK   (2 miles, 3km)

The River Lee Navigation begins at Bow Locks, and this is the obvious place to start exploring this waterway. You might come by walking along the Limehouse Cut, as many of the barges would have done instead of navigating the winding tidal Bow Creek. *The nearest station is Bromley-by-Bow (Underground – District line) via Lea Walk Bridge (Bridge 2).* Bow Locks are two chambers side by side, ie a double lock. There are two footbridges over Bow Locks. The smaller black iron one links the sides of the locks and is for the use of boaters and lock staff. A larger concrete footbridge carries the towpath over the locks to a long, thin island between the Lee Navigation and the tidal Bow Creek, which flows further inland. On the bridge, look behind you for a splendid view of the Canary Wharf and other tall buildings on the Isle of Dogs.

From the footbridge at Bow Locks, walk beside the canal following signs that say Leaway North and the Lea Valley Walk. Just beyond the green painted railway bridge is an entrance to the Bow Back Rivers. These are a 5-mile (8km) maze of semi-tidal channels between Bow and Stratford. They were heavily silted with two impassable locks. The Channel Tunnel Rail Link, which opened in 2007 at nearby Stratford, and the 2012 Olympic Games in London's East End brought major improvements to these muddy backwaters. The continued development is turning the Bow Back Rivers into a place to walk in green spaces as well as to watch football and other sports. Footpath access is most direct from Old Ford Lock (see page 110), but there is a path across Three Mills Island that leads to the Jubilee Greenway and the southern end of the Olympic Park.

Three Mills is a gem of industrial architecture and is one of the finest groups of waterside buildings in London. The House Mill, built in 1776, is the oldest and largest tidal mill in Britain. It used to grind grain for gin distilleries and visitors can see its milling machinery and waterwheels. The House Mill is open to the public

Three Mills.

on Sunday afternoons from May to October and has guided tours. The Clock Mill, which dates back to 1817, has a timepiece in the tower, making it the most prominent of the Three Mills complex. The tide mill worked by allowing incoming tidal water to flow upstream and then holding back the ebb tide water by use of flood gates. When the downstream water level dropped, the flood gates opened and the onrushing water turned the mill wheel. The third mill was probably a windmill that has long gone.

At Three Mills, the towpath crosses the canal on Bridge 4 to the west bank. On the east bank, a new public space is being created for markets and events around Three Mills. A tall hotel towers above the A11 Bow Flyover ahead. This is where Bow Bridge once stood. It was built in the 12th century on the orders of Matilda, wife of Henry I, after Matilda and her retinue nearly drowned when crossing the Lea at Old Ford on their way to Barking Abbey. Beyond the flyover, cross over the canal back to the east bank on a footbridge near one of the entrances to the Bow Back Rivers.

After a short featureless section, where redevelopment in 2021 was at a very early stage, you come to two large pipes and a bridge (Bridge 9) crossing the canal above your head. This is the

Northern Outfall Sewer, designed by Joseph Bazelgette and built in 1862–63 following the Big Stink of 1858. The bridge carries the Jubilee Greenway (see page 70), which joins the Capital Ring long distance path at this point. Pass under the bridge and Old Ford Lock lies ahead. On the right-hand side is a channel into Bow Back Waters with a towpath that goes to the London Stadium, now home to West Ham Football Club. Beyond lies the Queen Elizabeth Olympic Park. From here it is possible to explore most of the Bow Back Rivers on foot.

Cross the side channel to Old Ford Lock (not to be confused with the one on the Regent's Canal). The lock house was the headquarters of *The Big Breakfast* television programme for ten years and had a very colourful garden with a giant teacup. Sadly, this closed in 2002 and the garden is not open to public viewing. Like its namesake on the Regent's Canal, the lock stables remain as evidence of the old days on the canal. This section of the Lee Navigation can be badly affected by floating duckweed, caused by an accumulation of nutrients from drains that can make the water surface resemble a bowling green all year round. Periodically, the lock is closed for a day while the weed is removed.

The junction with the Hertford Union Canal appears on the left soon after the lock. The cafés on the boats and stalls on the land by the towpath offer refreshment in a cheerful street scene at the Sweetwater Trade Moorings. There are more conventional bars and restaurants on the opposite bank around the entrance to the Hertford Union Canal (see page 95), reached by crossing the Carpenters Road Bridge (Bridge 11). On the towpath side beyond the bridge was Hackney Wick Stadium, a famous venue for greyhound racing. During the 2012 Olympic Games, the site was the location for a media centre. Now there is a school, a London base for Loughborough University, shops and offices. *Carpenters Road Bridge and White Post Lane will take you to Hackney Wick station (London Overground – North London line).*

A WALK AROUND THE OLYMPIC PARK
(4 miles/6.5km around the edge of the park)

▲ *Olympic Park.*

There is much to see in the 560 acres of the Olympic Park. It is 1½ miles long and ½ mile wide (2.5km by 1km), with a network of paths that take about 2 hours to explore. If you start from the Lee Navigation at Old Ford Lock, the path runs into the park beside the River Lea. The large London Stadium, which was the centre of the 2012 Olympic Games, appears in front of you and will be a useful landmark on your walk. To see the scale of the park, continue northwards, crossing the River Lea and Carpenters Road (*the way in from Hackney Wick station*) to reach the Waterden entrance to the Queen Elizabeth Olympic Park. Continue along Middlesex Way or go down one of the paths leading to the river. You can cross the river to the huge velodrome and return on the east side where there are gardens, wildlife areas, playgrounds and a café for your delight and comfort. If you stay on the east side, you can reach the Westfield Stratford City shopping centre (*Stratford station: DLR; London Overground and Underground – Central line*). If you cross back to the west side and stay close to the river, you will pass Carpenters Road Lock, the most modern lock on the English waterways. More gardens and playgrounds lie ahead, where there are refreshments, toilets and an information point, but your eyes will be drawn to the tall helical ArcelorMittal Orbit, the world's longest tunnel slide. Down on the Waterworks River there are tour boats and craft for hire. Up on the bank in front of Stratford City is the Aquatic Centre. To complete a circular walk back to Old Ford Lock, go along Sidings Street and Marshgate Lane on the south side of the London Stadium.

HACKNEY WICK TO TOTTENHAM HALE
(3 miles, 5km)

After Eastway and the A12 road bridges, the canal has green spaces on the towpath side and residential buildings on the offside. The first green space is Wick Woodland, a peaceful place to wander amid 25 acres (10 hectares) of mature trees. Next comes Hackney Marshes, one of the largest areas of common land in London (336 acres/136 hectares) – large enough for 88 football pitches and plenty of room for other sports. Many famous footballers developed their skills here. The marshes became grassland following extensive drainage over the centuries and were established as a public open space in 1894. The third green space is a nature reserve created from former sewage works, the Middlesex Filter Beds. Only a few large lumps of concrete and some brick-lined depressions remain of the filter beds, but it is worth going in to look at the small island in the middle of the weir, where there used to be three mills: one for grinding flour, one for boring wooden pipes and the third for making pins.

After the Filter Beds, the towpath changes sides on a bridge that is all that remains of the Pond Lane Flood Gates. The flood gates originally were a half-lock, a single set of gates that could prevent high levels of water in the River Lea causing a flood in Hackney. The Pond Lane Flood Gates were of a vertical guillotine type. The gates became redundant after the building of the Thames Barrier and were removed in 1987. The towpath passes Lea Bridge Quay, home to the Docklands Canal Boat Trust, which has a boat that is fully accessible to people with physical disabilities. At Lea Bridge (Bridge 18), the Princess of Wales pub has a riverside terrace. The new Lee Valley Ice Centre is on the east side of the bridge. *The nearest station is Clapton, ½ mile (1km) away along Lea Bridge Road and Upper Clapton Road (London Overground line between Liverpool Street and Chingford).*

On the north side of Lea Bridge, the Capital Ring and the Lea Valley Walk continue together for the next mile to Horse Shoe

Bridge. The Lee Navigation takes on a more natural appearance, curving between grassy banks amid green spaces, starting at Millfields Park. At first there are modern apartment blocks on both sides but after the next footbridge (Wilton Point, Bridge 19) where the towpath crosses to the east side you will walk on the side of the Walthamstow Marsh Nature Reserve. This Site of Special Scientific Interest (SSSI) of 90 acres (37 hectares) is a set of flood meadows managed in the traditional way – shared as common land, grazed by cattle, mown for hay and fertilised by winter floods. The marsh was the scene of the first flight by a British aeroplane with a British engine, made by AV Roe in 1909. The workshop under the arches of the nearby railway bridge was the start of the AVRO airplane company. At the north end of the marsh, the towpath crosses back to the west side over Horse Shoe Bridge (Bridge 20) to Springfield Park.

Springfield Park is a popular spot for walkers, joggers and people who just want to sit and watch the boats go by. Leaside, the Sea Cadets base (TS Bulwark), is just downstream, while the Springfield Cruising Club Marina is on the opposite bank, and the very active Lea Rowing Club is a short distance upstream by the green painted footbridge (Bridge 21). The rowing club has a popular waterside café and there is car parking nearby.

The embankment enclosing Warwick Reservoirs appears on the offside of the river. This is the first of the 13 Lea Valley Reservoirs, which supply 10 per cent of London's water and stretch for 7 miles (11km) between here and Enfield. After a short section of housing on the towpath side, you will reach Markfield Park. The museum here has a restored beam engine that has been working since 1886. The engine was used for pumping sewage from Tottenham to the Beckton Sewage Treatment Works beside the Thames at Barking Creek.

Tottenham Lock has new housing with tower blocks on both sides. The development on the east side is on an island between the canal and the Coppermill Stream, which is a side stream of

A WALK AROUND BOTH SIDES OF THE CANAL AND WALTHAMSTOW MARSHES
(2–3 miles/3–5km)

An enjoyable circular walk can be made between Lea Bridge and Horse Shoe Bridge, going in one direction on a permissive path in front of the houses on the west side of the canal instead of crossing the footbridge at the north end of Millfields Park, before coming back on the towpath (1 mile/1½km in each direction). The walk can be lengthened by leaving the towpath to explore the paths in Walthamstow Marshes. Going up to the Warwick Reservoirs and back would add another mile.

The Lee at Walthamstow Marshes.

the River Lea. The name derives from a water mill that was used to make copper coins in the first half of the 19th century. The mill then became a water pumping station and is now the site of a water treatment works. Tottenham Hale, on the west side, is designed to have a village atmosphere at street level, with local shops and cafés. *Tottenham Hale station (National Rail to Liverpool Street; Underground – Victoria line) is nearby along Ferry Lane.* In the opposite direction, at Forest Road, there are paths by the reservoirs for walkers and birdwatchers.

TOTTENHAM TO WALTHAM CROSS (7 miles, 11km)

After Tottenham Lock, the navigation takes on a more rural aspect as it passes Tottenham Marshes. Stonebridge Lock is pleasantly situated and has a lively waterside café. At the car park there is a series of interesting mosaics made by local schoolchildren. Moorings stretch alongside the navigation on both sides of the lock. It is very popular with fishermen, which is not surprising on a river made famous by Izaak Walton's *The Compleat Angler* (1653). For the next 7 miles (11km), the canal runs nearly straight northwards following a line of large pylons. *If you want to break it into shorter walks, the railway has intermediate stations at Angel Road, Ponders End and Enfield (National Rail – Liverpool Street to Hertford line).*

The towpath changes to the east side at Stonebridge Lock and this gives access to wilder parts of Tottenham Marshes. Beyond the next footbridge, you pass into an industrial area that once was the centre of a thriving furniture industry, with timber yards and factories alongside the navigation. Near the viaduct that carries the North Circular Road (A406) over the Lea Valley, a new power plant is being constructed. This is the North London Heat and Power Project at Edmonton Eco Park, which recovers useful materials from waste and burns the rest to make energy and heat. *A sign at the towpath gives directions to Angel Road station at the western end of the viaduct.*

Markfield Beam Engine Museum.

The next 3 miles (5km), up to Enfield Lock, are flanked on the towpath side by the banks of two huge reservoirs, William Girling and King George's, that are popular with birdwatchers. At Pickett's Lock, the Lee Valley Leisure Centre on the offside has a golf course, camping site and a large undercover recreational complex that includes a multi-screen cinema. Unfortunately, there is no mooring for boats and no bridge for pedestrians from the towpath. Pickett's Lock is a single lock that was never converted to doubles like the others on the navigation.

At Ponders End Lock, South Island Marina is on the offside in a side stream that makes the island. *Ponders End station (National*

Lee Navigation.

Rail from Liverpool Street) is a short distance along Wharf Road by the marina. A large pub called The Navigation is on the offside next to the Lea Valley Road (A110) Bridge.

After this, Brimsdown Business Park dominates the offside of the navigation all the way to Enfield Lock, where the Canal & River Trust has offices and a maintenance yard. The famous Royal Small Arms Factory founded in 1818 was on the east side of the canal. This factory made the Lee-Enfield rifle used by British soldiers in the Second Boer War and the First and Second World Wars, leading the way in mass production and quality control techniques. The factory site has become the Enfield Island Village, which can be reached by the Ordnance Road Bridge. It is worth a walk around the village, where you will find lots of information about its history.

The towpath crosses the canal at Enfield Lock and remains on the west bank up to and beyond Waltham Cross. National Cycle

Gunpowder Mill at
Waltham Abbey.

Route 12 and the London Loop also cross this small bridge. You
pass The Greyhound pub before the modern bridge at Ordnance
Road. *Turn left (westwards) if you wish to go to Enfield Lock station.* On
the towpath, Rammey Marsh will be beside you until you reach
the lock that bears its name. At the lock is a charming display of
the artwork by children at the Prince of Wales Primary School in
Enfield. On the opposite bank of the lock is the Rammey Marsh
Cruising Club, which has a café open nearly all and every day.
After the M25 motorway, the canal approaches Waltham Abbey,
where there is Hazlemere Marina and Waltham Town Lock.
There is a lot of green open space here and it is an appropriate
place to end the walk. *Turn left along Station Road to reach Waltham
Cross station (National Rail from Liverpool Street).*

A WALK TO WALTHAM ABBEY   *(1 mile/1.5km there and back)*

With your back to Waltham Town Lock, turn left along the main road. The entrance to the Royal Gunpowder Mills is immediately on your left. Explosives have been made in buildings spread throughout its 175 acres (71 hectares) since 1665. It has its own internal canal system among woodland. It is now a Site of Special Scientific Interest (SSSI) and is home to the largest heronry in Essex. The mills are open to the public daily from May to October, and there is a Guy Fawkes display at the beginning of November.

▲ *Waltham Abbey Church.*

Cross the road and keep going straight ahead towards a roundabout. The Abbey Church is now visible. Proceed along Highbridge Street to the entrance. The Abbey Church was founded in 1030 but only the Norman nave and aisles still remain. The gardens are reputed to have been the burial place of King Harold after the Battle of Hastings in 1066. The Greenwich Meridian Line passes through a specially planted rose garden. The Lee Valley Information Centre is in the abbey grounds and the Cornmill Meadow Dragonfly Centre is nearby. There are plenty of pubs and cafés in the vicinity of the Abbey Church.

▲ *King Harold's burial place at Waltham Abbey.*

This could be combined with a walk down to Enfield Village Island via Gunpowder Park, returning by the towpath (3 miles/5km there and back). From the abbey, walk towards the river and take the first major road on the left, Meridian Road, before the McDonald's restaurant. This road goes under the M25 beside the River Lea. Where the road curves to the left, continue straight on a grassy path parallel to the river. This will bring you into Gunpowder Park, a large expanse of grassland that was once a testing ground for explosives. A hard-surfaced path continues southward beside the river until you reach a path that crosses the river and takes you to Enfield Village Island. Information boards in the village should help you to find the canal.

Some other London waterways

A rash of speculative canal building took place at the beginning of the 19th century, following the success of earlier canals. Many grandiose schemes proved to be financial failures and London had its share of unsuccessful waterways, now abandoned.

The **Croydon Canal** was part of a scheme to link London Docks with Portsmouth. Opened in 1809, it left the Thames by Surrey Docks and had 28 locks in the first 5 miles (8km) from Deptford. It reached Croydon at a point now occupied by West Croydon station. In parts it was a pretty canal but commercially it was a failure. The company sold out in 1836 to the railway company, which laid its track along the route of the canal. All that remains is a short stretch in Betts Park, Anerley.

The **Grand Surrey Canal** opened in 1810 from the Thames to Camberwell with a later branch to Peckham. It has totally vanished under road and building schemes.

The **Grosvenor Canal** left the Thames east of Chelsea Bridge and ran for ½ mile (1km) to a basin. The canal extended an existing creek and became navigable around 1824. It carried coal and stone and took away rubbish. The basin disappeared under Victoria station in 1860. Later the canal was shortened to a dock by Chelsea Bridge where rubbish was loaded into barges.

The **Kensington Canal**, built in 1828, ran from Chelsea Creek to a basin where Kensington Olympia now stands. In 1839 it was taken over by the West London Railway Company, which built a line northwards to link with the main line. Both canal and railway were a financial disaster and in less than a year the railway was leased off. The company operated at a loss for 20 years – a railway company without a railway, running a canal. Finally, the canal was converted to a railway between the basin and King's Road, Chelsea. Chelsea Creek is all that is left of the Kensington Canal.

The **Fleet** was a navigable river in the 12th century and became a canal in the 17th century. Its problems were continual silting and the ancient practice of using it as a rubbish tip. It was navigable as far as Holborn and was crossed by several fine bridges designed by Christopher Wren. It was actively dredged in the 17th century. Nothing remains of the canal, and the river is now an underground drain.

The **City Canal** on the Isle of Dogs was built on a huge scale as a ship canal but was only 193 feet (59m) long. It was no more than a large dock with a lock at either end. It became part of the West India Docks and is now under the shadow of Canary Wharf.

Conclusion

The image of canals, especially those passing through urban areas, has changed completely over the past few years. In London, commercial use of the canals has virtually finished as far as carrying bulk cargoes is concerned. The factories that grew on the canal banks stopped using water transport in favour of road and rail. Wharves, once busy loading and unloading goods and raw materials, became dusty storage places for pallets and redundant equipment. Soon many manufacturing companies moved their factories out of the capital because of the soaring costs of operating inside London. In many cases they have been replaced by acres of anonymous warehousing or redeveloped for residential purposes, but their history remains.

A few decades ago, a property adjacent to a canal was not regarded as a saleable asset by most estate agents. Now, in London, the canal is an integral part of new multi-million-pound developments. Use of the towpath is encouraged and information boards have sprung up everywhere. The Canal & River Trust has brought fresh management and harnesses the enthusiasm of volunteers. Local community groups are active in removing litter, displaying artwork and sharing the history of the canals. The authorities accept that residential boats can and should be part of these local communities. There is some way to go to stop the graffiti that spoils signs and information boards, and the casual dropping of bottles, cans and food containers is still a major problem. However, it is hoped that the public, and children in particular, will be educated to appreciate the asset in their midst.

A wonderful feature of London's canals is the way they connect green spaces – the parks, nature reserves, canalside gardens, playing fields and the small corners where wildlife can survive. The towpaths allow us to look and sometimes to enter. Go out there and see for yourself – there is a wonderful network of waterways just waiting to be explored in parts of London you hardly knew existed.

Further reading

BOOKS

Barton, Nicholas. *The Lost Rivers of London* 3rd edition. Historical Publications, 2016.

Bolton, Tom. *London's Lost Rivers: A Walker's Guide*. Strange Attractor, 2011.

Burton, Anthony. *Canal 250: The Story of Britain's Canals*. History Press, 2011.

Burton, Anthony. *The Canal Pioneers: Canal Construction from 2500 BC to the early 20th Century*. Pen and Sword Transport, 2017.

Burton, Anthony, and Pratt, Derek. *The Anatomy of Canals: The Early Years*. Tempus, 2001.

Burton, Anthony, and Pratt, Derek. *The Anatomy of Canals: The Mania Years*. Tempus, 2002.

Burton, Anthony, and Pratt, Derek. *The Anatomy of Canals: Decline and Renewal*. Tempus, 2003.

Burton, Anthony, and Pratt, Derek. *Britain's Canals: Exploring their Architectural & Engineering Wonders*. Adlard Coles Nautical, 2020.

Clayton, Anthony. *Subterranean City: Beneath the Streets of London*. Phillimore, 2000.

Conder, Tony. *Canal Narrowboats and Barges*. Shire, 2004.

Fathers, David. *The Regent's Canal*. Francis & Lincoln, 2012.

Fathers, David. *London's Lost Rivers: A Walker's Guide to the Subterranean Waterways of London*. Francis & Lincoln, 2017.

Fisher, Stuart. *The Canals of Britain: The Comprehensive Guide* 3rd edition. Adlard Coles Nautical, 2017.

Lansdell, Avril. *Canal Arts and Crafts* 2nd edition. Shire, 2004.

Pratt, Derek. *Waterways Past and Present*. Adlard Coles Nautical, 2006.

Pratt, Derek. *The Thames*. Adlard Coles Nautical, 2008.

Pratt, Derek. *London's Waterways*. Adlard Coles Nautical, 2010.

Sergeant, John, and Bartley, David. *Barging around Britain: Exploring the History of our Nation's Canals and Waterways*. Penguin, 2016.

Smith, Peter L. *Discovering Canals in Britain* 4th edition. Shire, 1993.

Talling, Paul. *London's Lost Rivers*. Random House, 2011.

Ware, Michael E. *History in Camera: Canals and Waterways*. Shire, 1987.

Winn, Jasper. *Water Ways: A thousand miles along Britain's Canals*. Profile Books, 2020.

MAGAZINES

Canal Boat, Kelsey Media.
www.canalboat.co.uk

Waterways World, WW Magazines.
www.waterwaysworld.com

Useful addresses

Canal & River Trust Little Venice office,
The Toll House, Delamere Terrace,
London W2 6ND. Tel: 0303 0404 4040.
Email: enquiries.londonsoutheast@
canalrivertrust.org.uk
www.canalrivertrust.org.uk

Friends of Grand Union Canal (Facebook
group) www.friendsofgrandunioncanal.
co.uk, www.facebook.com/groups/
friendsofgrandunioncanal

Friends of Slough Canal Tel: 07542 168444.
www.friendsofsloughcanal.com

Horsenden Hill, Horsenden Farm, Horsenden
Lane North, Greenford UB6 7PQ.
www.horsenden.co.uk

Inland Waterways Association, Island
House, Moor Road, Chesham HP5 1WA.
Tel: 01494 783453. www.waterways.org.uk

Jason's Trip, 42 Blomfield Road, London W9
2PF. www.jasons.co.uk

Jubilee Greenway www.tfl.gov.uk/modes/
walking/jubilee-greenway

Lee Valley Regional Park Authority,
Myddelton House, Bulls Cross, Enfield
EN2 9HG. Tel: 08456 770 600.
www.leevalleypark.org.uk

London Canal Museum, 12–13 New Wharf
Road, King's Cross, London N1 9RT. Tel:
020 7713 0836. www.canalmuseum.org.uk

London Waterbus Company, Camden Lock
Market, London NW1 8AF. Tel: 020 7482
2550. www.londonwaterbus.com

Packet Boat Waterside and Marina
(Aquavista), Packetboat Lane, Cowley,
Uxbridge, UB8 2JJ. Tel: 01895 449851.
www.aquavista.com/find-a-marina/
packet-boat-waterside-marina

Perivale Wood Local Nature Reserve,
Sunley Gardens, Perivale, Greenford
UB6 7PE. www.selbornesociety.org.uk/
perivale-wood

Ragged School Museum, 46–50
Copperfield Road, London E3 4RR.
www.raggedschoolmuseum.org.uk

Royal Gunpowder Mills, Beaulieu Drive,
Waltham Abbey, EN9 1JY. Tel: 01992 707370.
www.royalgunpowdermills.com

Royal Small Arms Factory, RSA Island
Centre, 12 Island Centre Way, Enfield EN3
6GS. Tel: 020 8482 2281. www.rsaf.org.uk

Thames21, Main Office: The City of London,
Guildhall, PO Box 270, London EC2P 2EJ.
Tel: 020 7248 7171. Satellite Office: The Lock
Office, Bow Locks, Navigation Road (off
Gillender Street), London E3 3JY.
Tel: 020 7515 3337. www.thames21.org.uk

The Pirate Castle, Gilbey's Wharf, Oval Road,
London NW1 7EA. Tel: 020 7267 6605.
www.thepiratecastle.org

Three Mills, The House Mill Trust,
The Miller's House, Three Mill Lane,
Bromley-by-Bow, London, E3 3DU.
Tel: 020 8980 4626. www.housemill.org.uk

Walker's Quay (Jenny Wren Canal Boat
Cruises), 250 Camden High Street, London
NW1 8QS. Tel: 020 7485 4433.
www.walkersquay.com

Waltham Abbey Church Centre, Abbey
Farmhouse, Abbey Gardens, Waltham
Abbey, E9 1XQ. Tel: 01992 767897.
www.walthamabbeychurch.co.uk

Zoological Society of London (ZSL), London
Zoo, Outer Circle, London, NW1 4RY. Tel:
020 7722 3333. www.zsl.org/zsl-london-zoo

Index

Acton Power Station 52
Acton's Lock 94
Adelaide Dock 25
Agar, William 69–70, 84
Albert Bridge 6
Alperton 56
aqueducts 24, 36, 53, 54–5
ArcelorMittal Orbit 111
Asylum Lock 24
AVRO airplane company 113

Bagley Walk 84–5
Ballot Box Bridge 57
Bartlett Park 102
Battlebridge Basin 88
Bazelgette, Joseph 109–10
Bixley Triangle 25
Blackberry Corner 24
Blow-up (Macclesfield) Bridge 76–7
Boston Manor Park 19
Bow Back Rivers 108, 110
Bow Bridge 109
Bow Locks 100, 108
Bow Wharf 95
Braunston, Northamptonshire 18
Brent, river 14, 21, 22, 53
Brent Creek 14, 16
Brent Reservoir (Welsh Harp) 53
Brent River Park 21, 24
Brent Valley Park 23
Brentford Gauging Locks 17, 18
Brentford Lock 14
Brentford Railway Dock 16
Brentford Transhipment Depot 17
brickfields 27, 36, 37, 50, 59, 61, 63
bridges 56
    cast-iron 19–20, 49
    humpback 25

roving 19–20, 32, 80–1
Brindley, James 48
Browning, Robert 46
Brunel, Isambard Kingdom 23, 24, 43, 51
Bulls Bridge 8, 25–6, 65
Bunny Park 23
Burton, Decimus 78

Camden Catacombs (Dead Dog Tunnel) 80
Camden Lock (Hampstead Road Locks) 31–2, 46–7, 70, 80–5
Camley Street Natural Park 84
Canal & River Trust 11, 18, 25, 48, 118, 123
canals
    history of 7–11, 14–15, 36, 40–4, 68–70, 100–1, 107
    maps 9, 14–15, 40–1, 68–9, 100–1, 106
Canalway Cavalcade 47
Capital Ring Path 16–17, 57, 110, 112–13
Carlton Bridge 49
Carpenters Road Bridge 110
Carpenters Road Lock 111
Channel Tunnel Rail Link 108
Chelsea Creek 121
City Canal 122
City Road Basin 92
City Road Lock 89, 90–1
Clitheroe's Lock 19
Clock Mill 109
Coal Drops Yard 84–5
Colne, river 36
Colne Brook 36
Colne Valley Trail 32, 36, 37
Colston Bridge 27

Congreve, William 70
Coppermill Stream 113–16
Cornmill Meadow Dragonfly Centre 120
Cowley Lock 25, 30, 31–2
Cowley Peachey Junction 28–9
Cowley Recreation Ground 31
Cowley Trail of Discovery 31
Crane, river 64
Crocker, Frank 72–3
Croydon Canal 121
Cumberland Basin 79

Dead Dog Tunnel (Camden Catacombs) 80
Denham Deep Lock 33
Docklands Canal Boat Trust 112
Docklands Light Railway (DLR) 96–7
Dog Rose Ramble 64
Duckett's Canal (Hertford Union Canal) 95, 110

Elthorne extension 21
Enfield Island Village 118, 120
Engineers Wharf 62

Fan Bridge 42, 44
Fellows, Morton & Clayton 32, 92
Fleet, river 122
Friends of the Grand Union 53–6

Gade, river 88
Gallows Bridge 19–20
Glade Lane Canalside Park 24
Glaxo Smith Kline (GSK) building 18–19
Grand Junction Canal 7–8, 14–15: see also Paddington Canal

Grand Junction Canal Company 10, 70
Grand Surrey Canal 121
Grand Union Canal 8, 11, 14–33, 53
  Brentford to Hanwell 16–24
  Hanwell to Hayes 24–6
  Hayes to West Drayton 27
  West Drayton to Denham 28–33
Grand Union Canal Company 25
Great Western Railway (GWR) 42–3, 49, 52, 64
Green Quarter, Southall 64
Greenford 58, 59, 60
Greenwich Meridian Line 120
Grosvenor Canal 121
Gruffalo Trail 57
Gunpowder Park 120

Hackney Marshes 112
Hackney Wick Stadium 110
Hampstead Road Locks (Camden Lock) 31–2, 46–7, 70, 80–5
Hanwell Flight of Locks 14, 22, 24
Harold, King 120
Hassell, John 50
Hawksmoor, Nicholas 102
Hayes 26, 50, 63
Helix Bridge 44
heronry 120
Hertford Union Canal (Duckett's Canal) 95, 110
Hillingdon Trail 62–3, 64
Homer, Thomas 68, 70
horse ramps 24, 48, 79, 84
Horse Shoe Bridge 112–13, 114
Horsenden Hill walks 57, 58
House Mill 108–9
Hydraulic Accumulator Tower 96–7, 101

Ice Wharf 81, 88
Inland Waterways Association (IWA) 47
Isle of Dogs 122

Islington Boat Club 92
Islington Tunnel 88–9

Jam 'ole run 64
Jason (public canal boat) 70
Jubilee Greenway 70–1, 94, 108, 110
Jubilee Meadow 24

Kensal Green Cemetery 51–2
Kensal Wharf (Port-a-Bella-Dock) 50
Kensington Canal 121
King's Cross Centre 84
Kingsland Basin (now Reliance Wharf) 94

Laburnum Bridge 94
Ladbroke Grove 50
Langley Country Park 37
Lansbury, George 102
Lea, river 107, 111, 112, 113–16, 120
Lea Bridge Quay 112
Lea Rowing Club 113
Lea Valley Reservoirs 113
Lea Valley Walk 112–13
Lee Navigation 8, 11, 95, 100, 106–20
  Bow to Hackney Wick 108–10
  Hackney Wick to Tottenham Hale 112–16
  Tottenham to Waltham Cross 116–19
Lee Valley Information Centre 120
Lee Valley Leisure Centre 117
Lee Valley Pathway 107
Lee Valley Regional Park 107
legging 71, 88
Limehouse Basin (formerly Regent's Canal Dock) 96, 100
Limehouse Cut 95, 96, 98–103, 108
  Limehouse to Bow Locks 101–2

Lisson Grove 11, 73, 74–5
Little Venice 44–7, 84
locks 70
  double locks 84, 107, 108
  pound locks 7, 100, 107
  stables 94–5, 110
London Canal Museum 88, 89
London Loop 27, 32, 36, 118–19
London Waterbus Company 81–4
London Wildlife Trust 84
London Zoo 46–7, 76–9
Lord, Thomas 72
Lyons Dock 58

Macclesfield (Blow-up) Bridge 76–7
Maida Vale tunnel 71
Maiden Road Bridge 85
Markfield Beam Engine Museum 117
Markfield Park 113
Marnham Fields 61
Marylebone Cricket Club (MCC) 72
Maypole Arm 25
Meanwhile Gardens 50
Middlesex Filter Beds 112
Midland Railway Company 84
Mile End Park 95
Millfields Park 114
Minet Country Park 64
Misbourne, river 32
Morgan, James 70
mosaics 21, 32, 62, 94, 116
murals 32, 49

Nash, John 68, 69
National Cycle Routes 32, 37, 118–19
New River 107
North Circular Aqueduct 53, 54–5
North London Heat and Power Project, Edmonton Eco Park 116

Northern Outfall Sewer 109–10
Northolt and Greenford
    Countryside Park 59
Northolt Mosque 61
Norwood Top Lock 25, 31–2

Old Ford Lock
    Lee Navigation 108, 110, 111
    Regent's Canal 94–5
Old Oak Wharf 52
Olympic Park 71, 94, 108, 110, 111
Ordnance Road Bridge 118
Osterley Lock 20–1
Oxford Canal 7, 18

Packet Boat Marina 11, 29, 36
Paddington Basin 38, 41–3
Paddington Canal 7–8, 15, 25,
    31–2, 40–65
    Paddington to Willesden
        45–52
    Willesden to Horsenden 52–7
    Horsenden to Bulls Bridge
        58–65
Paddington Packet Boat 42–3
paper mills 88
Paradise Fields 58
Park Royal 53
Perivale Wood 58
Pickett's Lock 117
Pickfords Carriers 92
Piggeries 22
Pirate Castle boating centre 80
Pond Lane Flood Gates 112
Port-a-Bella-Dock (Kensal
    Wharf) 50
Praed, William 10

Queen Elizabeth Olympic Park,
    see Olympic Park

Ragged School Museum 96
Rammey Marsh 119

Regent's Canal 8, 10, 15, 24, 25,
    41, 68–97
    Little Venice to King's Cross
        70–85
    King's Cross to Limehouse
        88–97
Regent's Canal Company 95
Regent's Canal Dock (now
    Limehouse Basin) 96, 100
Regent's Park 67, 76
Reliance Wharf (formerly
    Kingsland Basin) 94
Rembrandt Gardens 46
reservoirs 53, 113, 116, 117
Rosemary Gardens 93–4
Royal Gunpowder Mills,
    Waltham Abbey 119, 120
Royal Small Arms Factory 118

St Anne's Church 102
St Mary Magdalene Church,
    Westbourne Green 48
St Mary's Bridge 44
St Mary's Church, Hanwell 23
St Mary's Church, Northolt 59
St Pancras Basin 84
St Pancras Lock 86–7
Seacourt, Mary 52
Slough Arm 25, 28–9, 34–7
    Cowley Peachey to Slough
        36–7
South Bucks Way 33
Southall 8, 64
Spikes Bridge 64
Springfield Park 113
stables 41, 81, 94–5, 110
Stockley Park 27
Stonebridge Lock 116
Stonebridge Park 53
Stort Navigation 95

Taylor Woodrow 61–2
Thames, river 7, 16, 100

Thames Lock 14, 16, 17
Thames Path 16
Three Bridges 24
Three Mills Island 108–9
tollhouses 17, 32, 48, 71
Tottenham Hale 116
Tottenham Marshes 116
Trellick Tower 49–50

Uxbridge 8, 14, 32

viaducts 23, 84–5, 116
Victoria Park 94, 95

Walker's Wharf 84
Waltham Abbey 119, 120
Waltham Abbey Church 120
Walthamstow Marsh Nature
    Reserve 113
Walthamstow Marshes 114–15
Walton, Izaak 116
Warwick Reservoirs 113, 114
Waterworks River 111
Welsh Harp (Brent) Reservoir 53
Wenlock Basin 93
Wennington Green 95
West Drayton 8, 27, 50, 56
West India Docks 122
West London Motor Cruising
    Club 57
Westbourne Green 48, 49
Wharncliffe Viaduct 23
Wick Woodland 112
Willow Tree Open Space 62
Willowtree Marina 62–3
Wormwood Scrubs 52
Wren, Christopher 122

Yeading Brook 64
Yeading Dock 63–4
Yeading Valley Park 64